M000216935

SMART MOVES

SIMPLE WAYS TO TAKE CONTROL OF YOUR LIFE

SMART
MOVES

TÉA ANGELOS

WILEY

First published in 2023 by John Wiley & Sons Australia, Ltd

Level 4, 600 Bourke St, Melbourne, Victoria 3000, Australia

Typeset in Liberation Serif 11pt/15pt

© TA Group Pty Ltd 2023

The moral rights of the author have been asserted

ISBN: 978-1-394-16047-1

A catalogue record for this book is available from the National Library of Australia

All rights reserved. Except as permitted under the *Australian Copyright Act 1968* (for example, a fair dealing for the purposes of study, research, criticism or review), no part of this book may be reproduced, stored in a retrieval system, communicated or transmitted in any form or by any means without prior written permission. All inquiries should be made to the publisher at the address above.

Cover design and stripe concept by Alissa Dinallo
Internal design and artwork (except where noted) by Chris Shorten/Wiley

Page 5, 179, 205, 207, 224, 227, 283: Brain image: © NotionPic/Shutterstock. **Page 41, 261, 297: Person standing; page 233: Person sitting:** © tiny_selena/Shutterstock. **Page 63: Friends:** © robuart/Shutterstock. **Page 110: Crowded office meeting; page 292: One-on-one office meeting:** © GoodStudio/Shutterstock. **Page 122: Woman in dress; page 126: Woman standing:** © GoodStudio/Shutterstock. **Page 123: Woman with phone; page 132: Woman with purse; page 305: Woman standing:** © Nadya_Art/Shutterstock. **Page 41: People at table; page 90: Woman walking; page 316: couple walking:** © robuart/Shutterstock. **Page 179: Woman meditating:** © VectorMine/Shutterstock. **Page 179, 283: Woman symbol:** © MarkZilla/ Shutterstock. **Page 213: Woman, casual; page 303: Friends:** © Bukavik/ Shutterstock. **Page 275: Woman in wheelchair:** © Flash Vector/Shutterstock.

Disclaimer

The material in this publication is of the nature of general comment only, and does not represent professional advice. It is not intended to provide specific guidance for particular circumstances and it should not be relied on as the basis for any decision to take action or not take action on any matter which it covers. Readers should obtain professional advice where appropriate, before making any such decision. To the maximum extent permitted by law, the author and publisher disclaim all responsibility and liability to any person, arising directly or indirectly from any person taking or not taking action based on the information in this publication.

SKYAAA9EF97-D089-484A-A3C7-58B5EE5FAE55_022823

I would like to pay my respects to the Traditional Custodians of the land on which I work and live, the Turrbal and Jagera people, and recognise their continuing connection to land, waters and community.

I pay my respects to them and their cultures; and to their Elders past, present and emerging.

I would also like to extend that respect to any Aboriginal and/or Torres Strait Islander people who may read this book.

*To the Smart Women Society community—thank you for your
never-ending support and for making this book possible.*

CONTENTS

ABOUT THE AUTHOR

Téa Angelos is the founder and CEO of Smart Women Society (SWS), one of the largest and fastest-growing online platforms helping a thriving community of hundreds of thousands of women get smarter with their money, careers, wellbeing and relationships. SWS is on a mission to empower women around the world with the knowledge, tools and confidence they need to take control of their lives and achieve their goals.

Ever since she was in high school, Téa has been teaching her peers how to create budgets and write their resumés. With degrees in both law and commerce, she has previously worked as a business consultant to large global companies and also owns a digital marketing business.

Téa is a passionate advocate for women and is highly sought after as an expert speaker and commentator on chart-topping podcasts and in national media publications such as *Mamamia*, Yahoo Finance, *body + soul*, *9Honey*, Channel 7, *Daily Mail* and *House of Wellness*. Her ability to simplify complex topics into engaging, actionable and easy-to-understand steps has led her to help the lives of thousands globally.

INTRODUCTION

No-one really prepares you for adult life.

Trying to excel in your career, manage your money, maintain your friendships, look after your physical and mental health, reply to all your emails and texts, stay hydrated, avoid burnout, invest for your future, set healthy boundaries, work on your goals, be happy and get enough sleep.

If you feel exhausted after reading the above paragraph, I'm with you.

It can feel like a never-ending juggling act.

Ever since I was in school, I have always been obsessed with breaking things down into simpler steps.

As a student and then as a university tutor, I would always draw simple graphics and flowcharts breaking down the topics we learned in class and summarising the key points we had to know for exams. I created copies of these breakdowns and shared them with my friends and students as study notes.

In university, I would help my friends write their resumés and cover letters to land internships and graduate jobs.

At work, I would always preach the importance of financial independence and show my colleagues of all ages the steps to create a budget in the break room at lunchtime.

Nothing beat the feeling of seeing the smile on someone's face when a topic finally 'clicked' for them.

 My approach has always been the same: practical, actionable and easy to understand. I break down complex topics into visual summaries and simple steps, so they are easily digestible and quick to learn and implement.

My goal when I started Smart Women Society was to implement this on a larger scale, breaking down a variety of topics across all areas of our lives, and help people just like you feel confident and empowered to achieve their goals.

This book is filled with ~~more than 130~~ tips and lessons I've learned along the way through my experiences, research and ~~working~~ with industry-leading experts.

I wrote this book to help you take control of all areas of your life. To show you how much potential and power you have. To make you feel empowered to level up in your finances, your career, your relationships and your overall wellbeing.

Before you get stuck into this book, I have one request: take action.

Read the tips and implement them in your life.

It may feel scary, but the hardest step is always the first one.

Don't let yourself in a year's time wish you had started a year ago.

Start today.

HOW TO USE THIS BOOK

This book is broken down into four sections:

- Money
- Career
- Wellbeing
- Love.

Within each section is a variety of chapters covering different topics and issues that many of us face every day. Each topic is short and filled with simple, actionable and easy-to-understand tips that you can implement straight away.

Consider this book as your go-to guide. It's your companion and starting point as you navigate various situations and different seasons in your life. Make it your own — write all over it, highlight parts, fold down the corners and do research to learn more about the topics that interest you.

You can read this book from start to finish or you can start at whichever chapter is most relevant or interesting to you. One month you may want to try some new productivity techniques, and another month, you may be more focused on boosting your self-confidence. Re-visit the chapters as often as you need.

I would love to hear about your progress: send us a DM on our Instagram (@smartwomensociety) or email me at hello@smartwomensociety.com.

You've got this!

MONEY

In this section:

I've made a lot of silly money mistakes in my time. Some of my 'highlights' (in no particular order) include:

- I once went to a new hair salon to get my hair cut and coloured. I didn't ask how much it cost before the hairdresser started, and when I got to the counter, it was $650. I was absolutely mortified but had no other option than to just pay it.

- I didn't realise that I had to actually cancel subscriptions after the free trial period and ended up wasting hundreds of dollars on random apps and streaming services I never used.

- As soon as I received an offer for my graduate role, I bought a very expensive handbag so I could 'look the part' on my first day. I wasn't starting the job for another six months and I had already spent a big portion of my first pay cheque.

- I was running late to an appointment and couldn't find a park, so I stopped in a loading zone outside. I came out 15 minutes later to a very hefty fine.

- I always thought I needed to 'treat myself' after a long week at work and would constantly buy random beauty items or new clothes to boost my mood. The man at the post office remembered my name from how often I was going in, and would snidely ask me: 'So what did you get this week?'

We're all human. We all make mistakes that we may not be particularly proud of. However, what's important is that we forgive ourselves for these past mistakes and learn how we can improve in the future. For many people, learning how to manage your money was never really taught when they were growing up. The beliefs and the behaviours that we have towards money usually stem from how we saw our parents and other people interact with money and what we saw in movies or on TV. Maybe you've always told yourself that money is 'too hard'. Or maybe you've convinced yourself that it's 'too late' to change your relationship with money. But you are far more capable than you think and there is no better time than today to take the first step to transform not only your money, but your life.

Remember, personal finance is just that — personal. We all have our own unique upbringings, privileges and backgrounds, and negatively comparing yourself to someone else's situation is a waste of your time. The only person you should be comparing yourself to is the person you were yesterday. If you focus on becoming just 1 per cent better every day, you will see huge progress over time.

You might be wondering: what does 1 per cent better even look like? One per cent better can include a variety of things such as working on your money mindset, forgiving yourself for past money mistakes, setting financial goals, creating a budget, paying off debt, being financially prepared for an emergency, knowing where your money goes every month, exploring ways to grow and invest your money, and learning how to shop smarter and avoid impulse shopping.

It may feel overwhelming, confusing or daunting, but remember that you do not have to change everything all at once. Pick one or a few things to focus on at a time and build systems and habits so it becomes a natural part of your life. When you feel like you have a good grasp of the topics, choose some more areas to work on, and watch your confidence with money grow. What matters is that you have decided to take control, transform your relationship with money and work towards becoming financially free.

Being financially free and independent is so important. The reason for this is that when you are financially independent, it allows you to make your own decisions without the influence or control of others. It means you can say 'no' and walk away from things that do not serve you. It means that you no longer stress about money or have money hold you back when making a decision. It means you have full control of your time and can live life on your own terms.

And probably more importantly, financial freedom gives you choice. It gives you the choice to quit a job that you feel trapped in and take your time finding a better one, end a toxic relationship or be there for your loved ones when needed. This is why it's so important to build positive money habits and have a plan for your money, so that you are never in a situation where you feel stuck, trapped or held back.

1

Laying the foundations

YOUR MONEY MINDSET

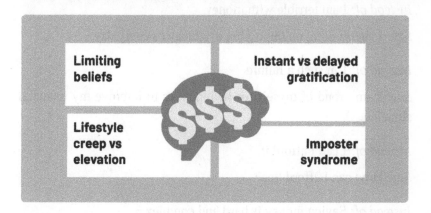

Limiting beliefs	Instant vs delayed gratification
Lifestyle creep vs elevation	Imposter syndrome

Our money mindset and attitudes towards money ultimately shape how we handle our finances. The money mindset we have is usually shaped by how we grew up around money, our experience with it growing up and witnessing how our parents and other people interacted with money. For example, if you come from a household where your dad handled all the finances and your mum didn't make any of those decisions, then this is likely to lead to you having similar beliefs as an adult. Or if money was always scarce and a source of stress in your household, this will impact how you handle money as an adult. Improving our money mindset comes from rewiring our limiting beliefs, educating ourselves about key financial concepts and strategies, and having open discussions about our financial goals and journeys.

LIMITING BELIEFS

A lot of people tend to have a range of limiting beliefs when it comes to money — that it's too hard or too complicated and they'll just never be good with it. These are the self-doubting thoughts that we tell ourselves that set limits on what we can achieve before we even start. The problem with holding these limiting beliefs is that it places a mental block on your ability to grow and develop a positive relationship with your money. Changing your self-talk around money is a major step in reframing your limiting beliefs into empowering beliefs.

Instead of: I am terrible with money.

Say: I am working on improving my finances every day.

Instead of: I'm such a failure.

Say: I am proud of myself for taking steps to improve my financial situation.

Instead of: I can't afford it.

Say: How can I afford this?

Instead of: Saving money is hard and complex.

Say: I break down my savings goals and automate them.

Instead of: Everyone else has so much more than me.

Say: I am on my financial journey.

Instead of: Why didn't I start earlier?

Say: I can't change the past, and there is no better time to start than today.

INSTANT VS DELAYED GRATIFICATION

Many of us are prone to wanting instant gratification: constantly buying new clothes to be 'trendy', wanting the latest thing to 'keep up' or seeking immediate results or pleasure. Even though choosing something now may feel good in the moment, taking a longer-term view and developing self-discipline can result in bigger and better rewards in the future. Delayed gratification is our ability to resist these temptations of instant pleasure, allowing us to stay focused on our long-term goals. It involves budgeting and spending mindfully, as well as developing discipline and patience to avoid impulse spending and decision making. Think about instant vs delayed gratification when you are developing your own financial goals. Consider whether your goals are focused on short-term gains or designed to look forward to a bigger picture.

LIFESTYLE CREEP VS ELEVATION

One of the biggest money mindset mistakes you can make is lifestyle creep. When you receive a pay rise at work or you increase your income with a new job or side hustle, it can be tempting to spend that extra money on a nicer car, more expensive restaurants or fancier clothes. Before you know it, these former luxuries become 'necessary' spending and you find yourself running out of money every month. Avoiding lifestyle creep involves having clear financial goals that you are working towards, tracking your spending and automating transfers to your savings and investments so they occur before any non-essential spending happens. When you receive an increase to your income, allocate a small portion to treat yourself and put the rest towards your financial goals.

In contrast to lifestyle creep, lifestyle elevation is the way we act following an increase in income that benefits our lives. Rather than seeing this as a negative, lifestyle elevation focuses on the positive benefit that can come from spending more on your lifestyle. This includes investing in personal self-care, spending more on higher quality items that will last longer, improving your standard of living, having the ability to travel and paying for convenience that frees up your time. Lifestyle elevation will align with your personal financial goals and values, whereas lifestyle creep will hold you back from achieving them.

IMPOSTER SYNDROME

We can often feel a sense of imposter syndrome when it comes to our finances. This includes feelings that we are not smart enough or good enough despite our experience, qualifications and achievements. Imposter syndrome can affect our finances in a variety of ways. It can cause us to not apply for a well-paid job that we are qualified for, not negotiate our salaries when starting a new role, not start investing or not pursue a promotion or business idea due to a fear of failure. Tracking your accomplishments and progress towards your goals is a great way to remind yourself of your abilities and how capable you are.

COMMUNITY STORY
Understanding my money story

When I turned 14, I got my first job at a fast-food chain. I enjoyed working as much as having the independence to spend money as I please. From age 14 to 19 I worked ... a lot. I remember receiving an almost $10000 AUD EOFY tax return at around 18 and I blew it all in just three months. Fast forward to age 20, I was living by myself, enjoying the life of an independent 20 year old ... except just living pay cheque to pay cheque.

My relationship with money finally started to shift when I got sick and had to stop working for a month. I was in a very bad mental space and all of my life problems hit me at once. It was the reset I needed for my life. Firstly, I realised that I wasn't actually living the life I wanted. Questioning who I really wanted to be, and the future I wanted to have, made me change my lifestyle.

As my everyday decisions changed, eventually I had to tackle money. I had been seeing an amazing kinesiologist for almost a year, and with just one session on my relationship with money, I had an awakening. She showed me that my relationship with money was deeply rooted in my self-worth, which was, for years, scarred by a broken relationship with my father. During my second therapy session, we unlocked that I subconsciously did not want to save up because I believed that if I saved my money, I wouldn't have a life. I saw my mom living frugally and not looking after herself just so that my brother and I could enjoy our lives.

After that session, I bought my first book about money and went on an Instagram and YouTube spree to find the best financial advisers. I am so grateful to have come across Smart Women Society, as their content is so easy to understand and is relatable in so many ways.

I'm only in the primary stages of building a healthy relationship with money and I love it already. I recently started a fortnightly, zero-based budget, setting up a savings account with interest, and enjoying seeing my savings grow. I've also reflected on my spending habits and a lifestyle I am happy with without all the frivolous stuff involved.

Thanks again SWS for all the work that you do.

Frances

FINANCIAL GOALS

If you find yourself feeling unmotivated or stuck when it comes to budgeting or saving money, you may not be setting effective money goals. Setting goals gives you a sense of direction and purpose for all the effort that you are putting into improving your finances. Without meaningful financial goals, we can lose interest or feel indifferent, which can result in bad money habits. Put yourself in the best position to take control of your money by defining your financial values and setting smart goals that align with these values.

Your money goals journey

HOW YOU THINK ACHIEVING YOUR MONEY GOALS GOES

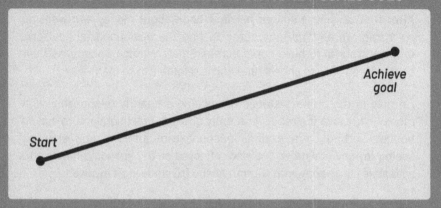

HOW ACHIEVING YOUR MONEY GOALS ACTUALLY GOES

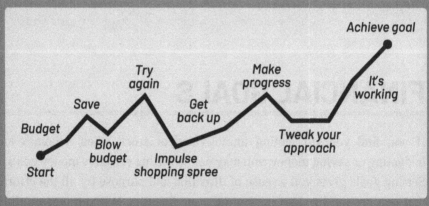

DEFINE YOUR FINANCIAL VALUES

Your financial values are the foundation on which the rest of your money journey is built. They are the guiding light that keep you on track with your goals and define the reasons why you set your money goals in the first place. Your financial values are the beliefs you hold on what is important. For example, you might value travelling and new experiences, or you might value stability and buying a home is your top priority.

The values you uphold will influence how you spend your money and decide on your long-term financial priorities. Think about what you value spending your money on. What brings you joy and fulfilment? What brings you comfort and security? Your financial values are not permanent, and they will change over time as your priorities and circumstances change.

CREATE YOUR FINANCIAL GOALS

Once you have defined your financial values, the next step is setting short-, medium- and long-term goals that align with these values. Think of what you want to achieve in the next year, next few years and well into the future and write out your goals using the SMART goals framework.

- **Specific:** Be really specific about exactly what you want to achieve. For example, your goal should be 'I want to save $5000 by the end of the year' as opposed to 'I want to save more money this year'.

- **Measurable:** Make sure your goals are measurable so you can track progress and success. For example, 'I want to pay off my debt in six months' or 'I want to save $3000 for my holiday in December'.

- **Attainable:** Dream big, but make sure your goals are still attainable and realistic. For example, it would be very difficult to save $50 000 a year if you earn $55 000. Your goals should be motivating but not unachievable.

- **Relevant:** Is this goal really what you want to achieve? How does this goal tie into your values and priorities in life? Having goals that are important to you will help you stay motivated to achieve them.

- **Time bound:** Set yourself a time period to achieve the goal. It's important to keep yourself accountable by setting a realistic deadline to achieve your goal.

BREAK DOWN YOUR GOALS AND TRACK YOUR PROGRESS

Once you have set your goals, break them down into smaller steps and milestones. If you have a yearly goal, think about what milestone you want to reach every quarter. If you have a monthly goal, think about what you want to achieve each week. Mark these milestones in your calendar and schedule check-ins to evaluate your progress.

STAY COMMITTED AND REWARD YOURSELF ALONG THE WAY

Achieving your money goals is never a linear path. Embrace the ups and downs of your journey and remember that small progress is still progress. What's important is that you stay consistent, resilient and remember the 'why' behind wanting to achieve your goal.

FIVE FINANCIAL NUMBERS YOU NEED TO KNOW

1. Your income
2. Your spending
3. Your debt

$

4. Your savings, investments and assets
5. Your net worth

If you want to take control of your finances, you need to know exactly where you stand at the current point in time and where you want to be. There are five financial numbers that you need to know: your income, spending, debt, savings/investments/asset equity and your net worth. Determining your current financial position will help you identify the areas where you are doing well, as well as the areas that need improvement. Tracking with these numbers over time will also show you the progress that you are making to help keep you motivated.

YOUR INCOME

Your income is any money that you receive on a regular basis. This will include your wages or salary, net income earned through a business, dividends or profit from your investments, interest from your bank, government payments, selling something you create or own, and any other notable positive money gain you receive. Relying on one source of income can be risky, especially if you are unexpectedly made redundant or have to quit your job. Instead, protect yourself by building multiple streams of income so you are less reliant on your wage/salary.

What you need to know:

- What are your income streams?
- How much money do you make on average from each of your income streams?

YOUR SPENDING

Your spending each month can be divided into essential and non-essential. Essential expenses are the things you need to spend money on each month to live, such as housing, bills, groceries and transport. Conversely, non-essential spending covers things like new clothes, eating out at restaurants and subscription services.

If you are unsure of your spending habits, print off your last two to three months of bank statements, grab two highlighters and go through each transaction line by line. Use one colour to highlight essential spending and the other colour for non-essential, discretionary spending.

What you need to know:

- How much do you spend each month?
- How much are your essential and non-essential expenses?
- For your non-essential spending, are there any areas you can reduce or cut down on?

YOUR DEBT

Your debt is the amount of money that you have borrowed from another person or party, which you owe back to them.

What you need to know:

- How much money do you owe and to whom?
- What are the terms of the debt, including the value, interest, payment due dates and any other obligations associated with the debt?

YOUR SAVINGS, INVESTMENTS AND ASSETS

Savings and investments include the money that you put into your bank account for short-term savings, longer-term savings, emergency funds, sinking funds or into investment accounts.

Your assets are the things that you own that have positive economic value. Your asset equity refers to the value of what you own in your assets. In other words, the total value of the asset minus any outstanding loan/debt you may have on that asset.

What you need to know:

- How much do you have in your savings accounts?

- How much do you have in your investment accounts?

- How much equity do you have in your assets?

YOUR NET WORTH

Your personal net worth is the combination of what you own (assets) and what you owe (liabilities). You should use your net worth to track your progress from year to year, and to hopefully see it improve and grow over time.

To calculate your net worth, calculate the total value of your assets. This includes the value of your home, value of vehicles, cash in bank accounts, value of investment accounts, value of bonds and any other notable asset that holds value. Then, calculate the total value of your liabilities. This includes the outstanding value of your mortgage, investment loans, credit card debt, car loan, personal loans and student loans. The difference between the two is your net worth.

What you need to know:

- What is the total value of your assets?

- What is the total value of your liabilities?

- What is your net worth (the difference between the total value of your assets and liabilities)?

SIGNS YOU ARE FINANCIALLY CONFIDENT

- You don't count down the days to your next payday

- You see money as a tool to help you live your best life

- You don't feel stressed/guilty when at a social event

- You don't transfer money out of your savings every month

- You are happy to pay for convenience/ make life easer

- You don't worry about a bill or payment coming in

There is no better feeling than being confident with and in control of your money. Financial confidence is about so much more than material things like buying flashy cars, eating at expensive restaurants or splurging on designer clothes and bags. It's about being in control of your money and not letting it control you. It's about not feeling stressed about how you will pay for things. It's about not having money hold you back from living your best life. We develop this confidence over time by adjusting our money mindset and implementing a money management system that helps us achieve our financial goals. As you start to take control of and change your relationship with your finances, you will begin to view money as a tool instead of a stressor.

2
Managing money

MONEY HABITS TO FOLLOW

Most good money habits do not come naturally — they are developed over time with consistent practice and a shift in mindset. Being good with your money is more than setting a new year's resolution and thinking that is all that's required to achieve your financial goals. Like any other positive habit, taking control of your finances is developed through repetition, diligence and focus. Here is a simple summary of actions that you can do daily, weekly, monthly and yearly to get better with your money.

DAILY

Track your spending	Check your bank account

WEEKLY

Weekly check-in	Plan your meals

MONTHLY

Review and update your budget	Automate your bills, savings and investments

YEARLY

Review insurances	Negotiate bills

'HAVING' A BUDGET VS 'BEING' ON A BUDGET

The term 'budget' has always seemed to carry a negative stigma with it. It is often misconstrued as something that is restricting, holds us back and means we can never have fun again. The truth is that a budget is simply a plan for your money. It helps you figure out where you are spending your money each month, making sure you have enough for all your bills while simultaneously planning ahead for your future and all the fun things you want to do.

There is also a huge difference between *having* a budget and *being* on a budget. This lies in whether you are in control of your budget or if you are letting your budget control you. *Being* on a budget feels very restrictive and revolves around always finding the cheapest option, cutting things out and spending the least amount of money possible. This is why many people 'give up' on a budget because they create one that is far too confining and rigid.

Having a budget, on the other hand, is all about creating a plan for your money that feels like a natural part of your life. It means working towards your financial goals and spending on things that matter most to you, so that money feels like a tool to help you live your best life and not something that holds you back.

Everyone's budget will be unique and there is no 'one-size-fits-all' rule for how you should allocate or spend your money. What matters is that you are taking care of your essential needs, aligning your spending with your personal values, and striking a balance between having fun in the present and preparing for your financial future.

HAVING A BUDGET		BEING ON A BUDGET
Creating a plan for your money that aligns with your financial goals and values	vs	Focusing on spending the least amount of money possible
Investing in quality items, spending on things that bring you joy and allowing yourself to still have fun	vs	Always choosing the cheapest option, cutting things out and not allowing yourself to spend on things you enjoy
Feels natural and allows you to live your best life	vs	Feels restrictive and holds you back from living your life
Flexible and sustainable	vs	Stressful and unsustainable

HOW TO MAKE A BUDGET

1. **Choose a tool**

2. **Determine the frequency**

3. **Plan ahead**

4. **Create your budget**

5. **Track your spending**

Working towards your long-term financial future does not require you to compromise living your life and having fun in the present. You can do both. A well-planned budget prioritises both your short- and long-term goals, making you feel confident and empowered with your money. Creating and updating your budget is not a time-consuming process. Once your base monthly budget is set up, you should only need to spend five to ten minutes a week checking in and making any updates.

Having a budget allows you to know exactly how much money is coming in and going out. It gives you the ability to identify any wasteful spending habits that could be better spent achieving your money goals. Budgeting will allow you to feel in control of your finances and keeps you accountable for your spending and saving. You can establish a strategy to achieve your financial goals while also setting aside money to pay your essential expenses and have fun.

There are three key components of a budget: your income, your expenses and your savings/investments. A budget is a plan for how you will allocate your income across your expenses (both essential and non-essential) and savings/investments.

CHOOSE A TOOL

Before we start, you need to select a budgeting tool. This can either be handwritten, a spreadsheet or through an app. I recommend using our

Wealth Building Dashboard budgeting spreadsheet (available from **smartwomensociety.com**) as it is super easy to use and update.

DETERMINE THE FREQUENCY

Before you start creating your budget, have a think about what frequency will work best for you. A budget is typically set monthly to best capture common income and expense payment cycles, but depending on your circumstances, a fortnightly or quarterly budget frequency may work best. No matter what frequency you select, be sure that all of your income and expenses are converted to a consistent frequency. For example: if you are budgeting fortnightly to align with your income payment cycle, convert your monthly phone bill to a fortnightly cost by using the formula:

(Monthly Bill × 12) ÷ 26.

PLAN AHEAD

When setting a budget, you need to plan for all of the known expenses that you will incur throughout the year. These may include bills that are paid quarterly, such as utility bills, or yearly, such as insurances or car registration.

While these costs aren't paid on a monthly or fortnightly basis, you can break them down into monthly components and make them a part of your regular budget, so that when the expense does roll around, you have enough money available to cover it. You don't want to have to transfer funds from your longer-term savings accounts or investment accounts to cover an insurance bill.

CREATE YOUR BUDGET

STEP 1: INCOME

Start off by writing out your after-tax monthly income so you know how much you have to work with. If you have a salary, this will be straightforward. But if you have a variable income that fluctuates, use your best estimate of how much money you will have coming in this month or use the average of your last three months of income.

If you have a variable income, calculate the minimum you need to earn each month to cover your rent/mortgage, bills, food, petrol and any other essential expenses. In periods of higher income, put away more money into your savings and emergency fund, to give you peace of mind during any quiet periods.

STEP 2: ESSENTIAL EXPENSES

Next, budget for all the essentials. These are all the things that you need to live each month, like your housing, bills, groceries and petrol. We will explore ways to reduce the cost of these expenses later.

STEP 3: YOUR FINANCIAL GOALS

After you've budgeted for the essentials, allocate a portion of your income towards your financial goals, such as additional debt repayments, savings and investments. Doing this before you budget for non-essential expenses ensures you are looking after future you.

STEP 4: NON-ESSENTIAL EXPENSES

All your remaining money is yours to spend on everything you love! A crucial part of your budget that is often overlooked is budgeting for fun. Look at your calendar for upcoming events or social commitments like birthdays or weddings, and budget for all aspects of them, such as transport, food, buying a gift or getting a new outfit.

Reflect on what you value and what brings you joy (whether that is dinners with friends or a coffee every morning from your local café) and make this a part of your budget. When you don't budget for fun and you make your budget too restrictive, you end up either just calling it quits on your budget or doing the dreaded transfer from savings to cover the expense, which will make you feel like you're never making any progress.

On the other hand, by planning ahead, accepting that you have some social events locked in and deciding that you want to prioritise fun, you can still put money towards your financial goals and spend money enjoying yourself. Budgeting for fun will make you feel like you have enough to do the things you want to do, while simultaneously prioritising future you.

> **TIP:** Automate as many payments as you can to make budgeting and managing your money as easy as possible. Some examples of things you can automate are bill payments, debt repayments and transfers to your savings and investment accounts. Putting things on autopilot means you can stay organised, save time and make sure you do not fall behind on the things that matter.

TRACK YOUR SPENDING

Lastly, make sure to track your actual spending throughout the month and see how it compares to your budget. Tracking your expenses highlights your spending patterns and gives you the knowledge of where your money is actually going every month. By tracking your transactions, you will see how quickly some of the smaller purchases can add up into large portions of your total spending. It also identifies any unknown costs that you may not be aware of, such as old subscription fees or account fees for services that you no longer use.

Being conscious of where your money is going makes you more accountable and trains your mind to question whether a purchase is really needed. Tracking your spending is not about questioning every small purchase you make; it is about being conscious of the spending you are doing and feeling in control of your money.

Review your budget at the end of every week and month and see if there are any areas where you overspent, underspent or had any unplanned expenses. Use your actual spending information to make tweaks to your budget.

BANK ACCOUNTS

How many bank accounts you have and how you set up your banking structure will vary depending on your personal needs and preferences. Typically, your bank accounts can be split into either spending accounts or savings accounts.

SPENDING ACCOUNTS

Set up an everyday spending account to have your salary paid into and to manage all your daily expenses, such as housing, bills, groceries, debt payments and transport. When looking for an everyday spending account, search for accounts with no account keeping fees, no minimum deposits and no overdraft fees. You may also choose to have a separate spending account for non-essential, 'fun' spending to keep this spending separate from your everyday essentials.

SAVINGS ACCOUNTS

There is no magic number of savings accounts to have. Some people prefer having one account to house all their savings, others prefer splitting it into two accounts for short-term and longer-term goals, and others like have multiple savings accounts for each individual goal. Choose a method that works best for you and set up automatic transfers from your everyday spending account into these savings accounts.

When looking for a new savings account, you should compare the following features:

- Interest rate: What is the rate and what is the frequency of payment? Is this a high-interest bank account?

- Account fee: Is there a monthly account management fee?

- Minimum or maximum balances: Is there a minimum or maximum balance required to receive the monthly interest?

Your Bank Accounts

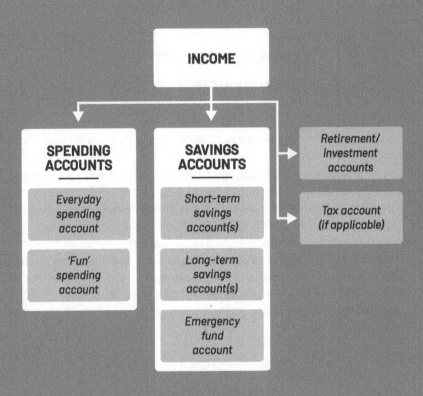

- Withdrawals: Is there a limit on how many times you can withdraw money from the account?

- Deposits: Do you need to make regular deposits to keep the account open or to gain the full interest rate?

An account that is a necessity is an emergency fund savings account. This account is typically held at a different bank from the one you do your daily banking with and serves as a safety net for unexpected situations. We will explore this account further in the next topic.

COMMUNITY STORY
Taking control of cashflow

I am a sole trader and have always struggled with knowing how much money to put away for tax and super. I got to tax time one year and realised I hadn't put the right amount away each quarter. This meant I had to come up with money that I had potentially already spent. I decided to change my habits. I put a percentage of tax away each pay in an account I can't access, along with a percentage to separate super, spend and save accounts. This really helps me monitor where my money is going and makes me think twice about whether I really want to buy something that I potentially don't have the money for at the time. I feel much more in control of where my money is going now, and rest comfortably at night knowing I won't be out of pocket at tax time.

Liz

EMERGENCY FUNDS

Life is unpredictable and unexpected emergencies and events are inevitable. Things like job loss, major health/dental expenses, relationship breakdowns, emergency pet care, car issues, home repairs and unexpected travel (for family emergencies etc.) have a way of randomly popping up when we least expect it. One of the most important bank accounts you need is an emergency fund. It is a savings account that also acts as a safety net. Having an emergency fund means that whenever an emergency occurs, you do not have to go into debt or worry about the money side of things.

HOW MUCH SHOULD MY EMERGENCY FUND HAVE?

Your emergency fund should ideally cover three to six months of living expenses such as housing, bills, groceries and transport. If you are just getting started with your emergency fund and your monthly living expenses are $3000, saving $9000 to $18000 can feel overwhelming. Instead, focus on saving $1000 as quickly as you can and then set aside a portion of your income each month as part of your budget to grow your emergency fund over time. Once you have saved an emergency fund that you are comfortable with, re-allocate this budget back to your other savings and investments. You should keep your emergency fund in a high-yield savings account, ideally with a different bank from your other accounts so that you are not tempted to spend it.

SHOULD I SPEND MY EMERGENCY FUND?

A flash sale at your favourite store is not an emergency. Neither is a friend's wedding that you have known about for months. You should only spend your emergency fund in proper emergencies.

To make sure you are spending your emergency fund for the right reasons, ask yourself:

- Is it necessary?
- Is it unexpected?
- Is it urgent?

After an emergency occurs, focus on topping your emergency fund back up to its full value.

QUESTIONS TO ASK BEFORE TAKING ON DEBT

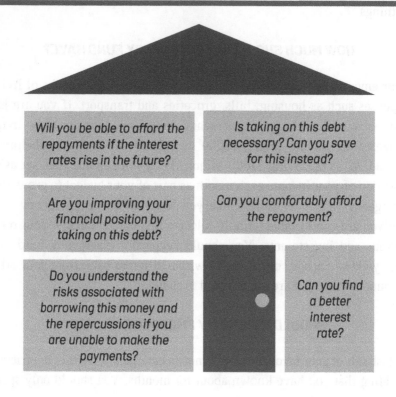

Will you be able to afford the repayments if the interest rates rise in the future?

Is taking on this debt necessary? Can you save for this instead?

Are you improving your financial position by taking on this debt?

Can you comfortably afford the repayment?

Do you understand the risks associated with borrowing this money and the repercussions if you are unable to make the payments?

Can you find a better interest rate?

An important personal finance principle is to spend less than you earn. What this means is that your expenses should not outweigh your income, otherwise you will need to go into debt to cover the difference. Taking on debt is a serious commitment, so it is important that you understand the circumstances and details surrounding a loan. Ask yourself the questions above before taking on any debt and make sure you are comfortable answering them all.

Not all debt is bad debt. Good debt will help you achieve your goals, whereas bad debt holds you back. Good debt can be described as debt you take on that assists you in generating more income or building your net worth. This debt is considered positive as it allows you to access money to help grow your financial position. This type of debt includes mortgages, starting a business or getting some form of education or training.

Bad debt, on the other hand, is considered negative as it involves borrowing money for consumed goods or services, depreciating assets and anything else that has no future value. If the purchase does not create income or build your net worth, it is likely bad debt. This type of debt includes credit card debt, buy-now-pay-later schemes, personal loans and high-value car loans. By minimising your bad debt, you will be able to re-allocate those funds into areas that will positively contribute to your money goals and personal wealth.

PAYING OFF DEBT

DEBT SNOWBALL

SMALLEST TO LARGEST BALANCE

Suitable for:
Multiple small debts

Pros:
- *Quick 'wins' – pay off small debts fast*
- *Helps build confidence and motivation*

Cons:
- *More interest paid overall*

DEBT AVALANCHE

HIGHEST TO LOWEST INTEREST RATE

Suitable for:
Mix of large and small debts with varying interest rates

Pros:
- *Less interest paid overall (saves you money)*

Cons:
- *Harder to stay motivated*

Accumulating and paying off debt can cause a great deal of stress. The regular payments build up and it can feel like a never-ending cycle trying to pay it off. Taking charge of your debts is one of the hardest but most rewarding things you can do with your money. Start off by making a list of all your debts. Write out all the terms of each debt, such as the value, interest rate, payment due dates and any other associated obligations. Next, choose a debt pay-off strategy that you want to follow. The two most popular debt pay-off strategies are the debt snowball method and the debt avalanche method. Each method has pros and cons, so pick the method that works best for you. If you want to pay off your debt faster, you need to contribute more money than the minimum repayment. Think of ways that you can increase your income or reduce your expenses to have more money to put towards your debt. The more money you can put towards your debt, the faster you will become debt free.

DEBT SNOWBALL

The debt snowball method focuses on paying off your debts in order from smallest to largest value. As you pay off each debt one by one, you roll over the payment you were paying on the smaller debt into the next-smallest debt. This strategy allows you to build momentum in your debt pay-off journey by removing these debts out of your budget and out of your mind. Saving money and paying off debt is as much a mental discipline as it is a mathematical equation. The debt snowball method builds on this idea and boosts your financial confidence with each debt that you pay off.

Steps:

1. Write out all of your debts from the smallest to largest dollar amount. Do not take into account interest rates.

2. Pay the minimum repayment amounts towards all of your debts, excluding your smallest debt.

3. Focus on paying as much as you can over the minimum repayment amount on your smallest debt.

4. Continue paying off your debts until the smallest debt is paid.

5. Once the smallest debt is paid off, use the money you were paying on the smallest debt towards the next-smallest debt.

6. Repeat this process until all of your debt is paid off.

DEBT AVALANCHE

The debt avalanche method focuses on paying off your debts from the highest interest rate to the lowest regardless of the balance. Similar to the debt snowball method, once you pay off each debt one by one, you roll over the payment you were paying on the highest interest debt into the next highest interest debt. This strategy prioritises tackling your 'worst' debt first. The debt avalanche method tends to be more difficult for people to stay committed to; however, it also leads to paying less interest in the long run. The core foundation of both methods is paying more than the minimum payment each month and building momentum to increase payments as each debt is paid off.

Steps:

1. Write out all of your debts from the highest interest rate to the lowest interest rate. Do not take debt value into account.

2. Pay the minimum repayment amount towards all of your debts, excluding your highest interest rate debt.

3. Focus on paying as much as you can over the minimum repayment amount on your highest interest rate debt.

4. Continue paying off your debts until the highest interest rate debt is paid off.

5. Once the highest interest rate debt is paid off, use the money you were paying on that debt for the next highest interest rate debt.

6. Repeat this process until all your debt is paid off.

PAYING DOWN A DEBT EXAMPLE

Let's say you had the following three debts:

- Debt 1: Credit card—debt value $2200; interest rate 17 per cent

- Debt 2: Personal loan—debt value $900; interest rate 11 per cent

- Debt 3: Car loan—debt value $14 400; interest rate 5 per cent

Using the debt snowball method, you would focus on paying the debts off in the following order: Debt 2, Debt 1 and Debt 3 (smallest to largest value).

Using the debt avalanche method, you would focus on paying the debts off in the following order: Debt 1, Debt 2 and Debt 3 (highest interest rate to lowest interest rate).

COMMUNITY STORY
My journey to becoming debt free

When I was 18, I got my first full-time job at the local grocery store. Not great, but it gave me so much disposable income and I LOVED it.

But I really wanted to buy my own house. I'd always loved looking at houses and clipping magazine pictures of my future home. So I thought I'd ask someone I trusted for advice on how I should go about it. I was told point blank that no-one would lend an 18 year old money to buy a house, no matter how much I earned. That I needed to get myself a credit card and then I'd have a credit rating and then I could get finance for a house. Fast track to my early 20s and I was in a lot of credit card debt!

So I pushed through and started to work at paying it off, got a consolidation loan and still couldn't get on top of the debt — with no house in sight. In my early 30s, I had my son and was 20k in debt. And that was the big kick in the butt I needed to get my debt under control. I started reading blogs and 'how to pay your debt' pins on Pinterest until I came across the snowball method.

Fast forward to my late 30s and I've bought my first home. I'm debt free — mortgage aside — and I don't own a credit card. I have a great budget, and I'm quite happy to say 'no' to something because I can't afford it. It's a huge mindset to change, but worth every sacrifice you make … and by sacrifice, I mean those shoes and bags and dinners out.

My takeaway from this? Don't get advice from anyone BUT professionals. Also, don't get a credit card or loan to pay off a credit card — it never works. Cap your debt and pay it down as fast as you can.

Jade

PAYDAY CHECKLIST

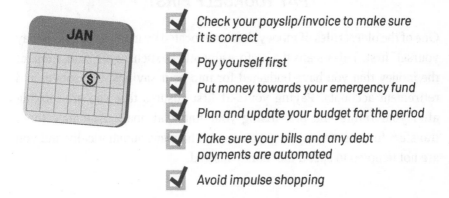

☑ Check your payslip/invoice to make sure it is correct

☑ Pay yourself first

☑ Put money towards your emergency fund

☑ Plan and update your budget for the period

☑ Make sure your bills and any debt payments are automated

☑ Avoid impulse shopping

Payday is an important day in your money calendar. Developing positive money habits requires a consistent routine, and your payday is a great opportunity to put these into action. Use the checklist above to help you navigate payday with ease.

CHECK YOUR PAYSLIP

No matter if you work for a big multinational corporation, a local business or are a sole trader/business owner, it is important that you check your payslips and invoices when they come in to make sure they are all correct. Both human error and computer error (or intentional error) can mean you are missing out on what you are entitled to.

You should also understand your superannuation (retirement) entitlements and check that the correct contributions are being made into your account. If you have student debt that your employer is required to pay on your behalf, make sure that this has been accounted for correctly. If you are paid hourly, your hourly rate and the number of hours you worked at that rate should be clearly stated on your payslip. Check for any loadings, bonuses or other allowances you are entitled to, as well as any other relevant deductions. If you are a sole trader/business owner, check that you have been paid the correct amount stated on your invoice for the goods or services you provided.

PAY YOURSELF FIRST

One of the oldest rules of money that is advocated by many experts is to pay yourself first. This means that before any other expenses are paid, transfer the money that you have budgeted for into your savings, investment and retirement accounts. Paying yourself first ensures that you are looking after your future and prioritising your financial goals. Automate these transfers for as soon as you get paid, so it happens automatically and you are not tempted to spend the money instead.

PUT MONEY TOWARDS YOUR EMERGENCY FUND

Your emergency fund is one of the most important bank accounts you need to help you navigate unexpected or unplanned events in life. Allocate a portion of your pay towards your emergency fund and automate this transfer for the day you get paid.

UPDATE YOUR BUDGET

Take a look at your budget and make any adjustments to account for any upcoming irregular expenses, social events or other known changes. By doing this, you can plan ahead to make sure you are not caught by surprise. You may also find that you have a surplus of funds for the pay period and can redirect this money to your debts, savings or investments.

AUTOMATE YOUR BILLS AND DEBT PAYMENTS

Keep a list of your regular bills and payments, and check the bills when they come in to make sure all details are correct. Schedule a reminder in your calendar or diary for when they are due, and set up automatic payments where possible to make sure you never miss a due date.

AVOID IMPULSE SHOPPING

Pay day is always the best day of the week/fortnight/month. It can be tempting to start spending all your pay because you feel cashed up, but often you'll regret it later when you realise that you didn't want or need any of it. Instead, allocate a portion of your budget for 'fun' spending like shopping and going out, and stick to this amount each month. Your future self will thank you.

MONEY CONVERSATION STARTERS

What is your earliest
memory of money?

Are you a natural
spender or saver?

What do you value
spending your
money on?

Do you create a
budget for
yourself?

What does being
financially 'comfortable'
look like to you?

What are your current
financial goals?

Talking about money can be scary, but it can also make you feel more empowered and motivated in your own financial journey. Having transparent conversations about money benefits us all. We learn more about the people around us, we pick up tips and strategies that we can apply to our own finances, and we can encourage each other to keep working towards our financial goals. Here are some financial conversation starters to try with your partner, friends, colleagues or family (don't forget to consider the context and your relationship with the person first).

MANAGING MONEY AS A COUPLE

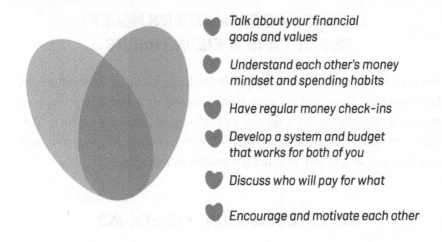

Talk about your financial goals and values

Understand each other's money mindset and spending habits

Have regular money check-ins

Develop a system and budget that works for both of you

Discuss who will pay for what

Encourage and motivate each other

Money is often a point of contention in relationships and can be a tricky topic to navigate. Effectively managing money as a couple relies on open and honest communication. Without communication, money-related issues develop into larger conflicts that are detrimental to the entire relationship. By being open, honest and willing to look at your money together through an objective lens, you can build trust in your relationship, avoid money arguments and make important decisions as a team.

TALK ABOUT YOUR FINANCIAL GOALS AND VALUES

It is important that you have open communication about your financial goals and values. You may have overlapping values, but also individual values. One person may value travelling and social activities, while the other prioritises personal care and education. Having these conversations is critical in understanding how you will manage money as a couple while also ensuring both people's needs are being met.

You should set short- and long-term goals both individually and as a couple. These goals will help form your budget and how you plan to spend your money.

UNDERSTAND EACH OTHER'S MONEY
MINDSET AND SPENDING HABITS

We all have different money stories and upbringings that have influenced how we think about and act with money. Spend time learning about your partner's relationship with money and talk openly about your own. This will allow you to better understand their mindset when it comes to money and how you would like to approach money as a couple.

HAVE REGULAR MONEY CHECK-INS

A money date is a time specifically set aside to discuss everything in your relationship that has to do with finances, from your day-to-day earnings and expenses to your short-term goals and long-term investments for retirement. Set up a regular date night with each other (it could be the first Monday of every month, for example), grab your favourite food and beverage of choice and chat openly about your shared financial goals, any issues you need to tackle and check in with your budget. Money is a massive point of friction for many relationships, so being on the same page is important.

DEVELOP A SYSTEM AND BUDGET THAT WORKS
FOR BOTH OF YOU

How you choose to manage your money as a couple is a personal decision and will come down to what works best for you and your partner. Some couples prefer having totally separate finances, others like to have everything combined and others have joint bills accounts and separate spending accounts. No matter the system, honesty and trust are integral in the success of managing finances together.

Newer couples or couples that do not live together or do not have many shared expenses may opt to keep their finances completely separate. In this scenario, the couple may take turns or split paying for expenses such as eating out or going on a trip. Over time, this system may cause tension if the distribution of spending is not equitable between both people.

Having combined finances makes managing your budget as a couple the simplest, but it relies on both people being comfortable with each other's money behaviours and respecting the goals they have set as a couple. When you have fully combined finances, it is a good idea to talk to your partner about how you will spend money and if there is a certain threshold for a purchase where you will need to consult each other first. For example, you may set a $500 threshold. This means that for any purchase you want to make over $500, you need to chat with your partner first before buying it.

A combination of joint and personal accounts provides a balance of budgeting efficiency, aligning your goals as a couple, but allowing for individual financial control.

You may decide to:

- put a percentage of your income into a joint everyday account for joint expenses, such as bills and groceries

- make contributions to your joint savings/emergency fund accounts

- keep a percentage of your income in personal spending accounts to spend however you wish.

In this scenario, joint expenses are accounted for together, but individual spending is kept separate.

Sit down with your partner and discuss what money management system will work best for you both. If you find that a system is no longer working for you, communicate with your partner and make adjustments where necessary. Remember, the way you handle your finances will be unique to you.

DISCUSS WHO WILL PAY FOR WHAT

Depending on your money system, you will need to make it clear how expenses will be split between you. This may be an equal 50/50 split across all joint expenses, or an equitable solution where the contribution is based on your respective incomes. You should also discuss who is responsible for making certain payments or paying certain bills to avoid any confusion or missed deadlines.

ENCOURAGE AND MOTIVATE EACH OTHER

Continuously encourage and motivate each other to work towards both your individual and shared financial goals. If your partner has not previously prioritised saving and is on a new money-saving journey with you, you will need to be patient as their money mindset is changing. Keep encouraging your partner, tell them that you're proud of them and remind them of why you have set those goals.

If you like getting competitive — do a savings challenge together. There have been lots of couples in the SWS community who print off one of our savings challenges and race to see who can finish it first. You can also get creative and suggest budget-friendly date ideas that are not costly, but still allow you to spend quality time together. This might include having a picnic, visiting a museum or art gallery, having a paint-and-sip night at home or having your own home spa day.

MOVING OUT AND NAVIGATING MONEY WITH ROOMMATES

Build a 'moving-out' nest egg

Set up your budget

Agree on a money strategy

Moving out for the first time is exciting, but equally scary. Having your own space and being in charge of paying bills and maintaining a home is a big step in becoming an adult, and there are many things that you will learn and discover along the way. You may be moving out alone, living with friends or with new roommates. Whatever situation you are in, managing the money side of moving out can be tricky. From creating a new budget, to furnishing your place and agreeing on a money strategy with roommates, there is a lot to consider. Follow the tips below to make the process as smooth as possible.

BUILD A 'MOVING-OUT' NEST EGG

Before moving out, save up a moving-out nest egg. Similar to an emergency fund, having a sum of money that can cover essential moving-out costs, such as buying appliances and furniture, as well as covering the first couple of months of bills will keep you on the front foot and avoid any stress if unexpected costs arise. If you have a plan to move out by a certain date, you can also slowly start buying essentials for your place so that it spreads out the expenses. Take advantage of sales periods or search online marketplaces for cheaper, second-hand options.

SET UP YOUR BUDGET

Prior to moving out, set up your budget to make sure you will be able to afford all of the changing and new expenses that you will experience. Forecast for all the shared utility household costs and set a budget for how much you would like to spend on individual expenses, such as groceries. Refer to the start of this chapter to help you get started. If you are planning on moving out for the first time or moving into a new space that will significantly increase your expenses, start living on this new budget before you make the move. By doing this, you can test if your new budget is realistic and liveable.

AGREE ON A MONEY STRATEGY

When you move in with a roommate or a group of roommates, you should establish a strategy for how the group and household finances will be managed. This should include agreeing on the bond responsibilities and paying shared utility bills (electricity, water, internet etc.), paying for shared household groceries (food, cleaning products etc.) and maintenance costs (lawn mowing, damaged appliances). Use payment sharing apps to help make managing shared costs quick and easy. There should also be an agreed strategy for withdrawing from the rental lease and the financial implications of this, including damage repairs, dealing with shared assets and notice periods. Don't forget to also discuss your strategy around household chores, especially in shared spaces around the house, and have open communication lines about your schedule and social activities.

3
Saving money

SAVINGS STRATEGIES

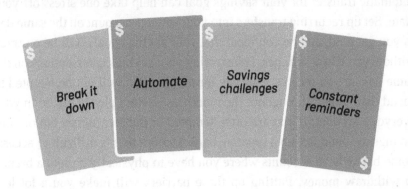

A big part of taking control of your finances is having clear savings goals that are aligned with your financial values. While the goal defines where you want to get to, it is the strategy that you implement that will make it happen. There is no one-size-fits-all approach when it comes to savings strategies—you may find automation works best for you or you may need to set more engaging challenges to stay motivated and bring out your competitive side. No matter the strategy, what matters most is that you stay consistent and transform the strategy into a subconscious habit.

BREAK IT DOWN

The most straightforward and common strategy is to break down your savings goal into smaller chunks that can be realistically incorporated into your monthly budget. It can be overwhelming thinking about how you are going to save a huge chunk of money, and this can make you feel deflated before you even start. By breaking the target goal down, it feels more realistic and achievable. For example, if you are wanting to save $5000 in 12 months, you need to set aside around $417 each month or $97 per week. The overall goal now feels more manageable as you are instead focusing on saving $97 consistently each week. You can also easily keep track of your progress as you hit milestones along the way.

AUTOMATE

With all of the other things we have to worry about in our day, setting up an automatic transfer for your savings goal can help take one stress off your plate. Set up recurring transfers into your savings account on the same day as you get paid, and be confident that your savings goals will be on track without you lifting a finger. Transferring your savings contributions on the same day as you receive your pay means that you will not be tempted to spend that money throughout the month as it won't physically be in your everyday account. If you are often tempted to transfer money out of your savings to spend, set up a separate bank account that is difficult to access. Some banks have accounts where you have to physically go into a branch to withdraw money. Putting up these barriers will make you a lot less likely to spend the money.

SAVINGS CHALLENGES

If you prefer being more actively involved in your savings progress, you can try gamifying your savings goal by doing a savings challenge. There are many templates you can print off for varying amounts and goal types (we have a free one on **smartwomensociety.com/free-resources**).

As you hit milestones or save a certain amount, you cross off or colour in the template. This is a fun way to stay motivated and make saving feel less of a chore. You can also challenge a friend or your partner to do it with you if you want an extra dose of accountability and competition.

CONSTANT REMINDERS

Surround yourself with constant reminders of your goal to help you stay on track along the way. If you are planning a holiday, set the destination as your phone wallpaper so you will see your goal numerous times every day when you pick up your phone. If you are saving for a house deposit, print a photo of your dream house and stick it up on your desk at work. Not only will this regular exposure keep you motivated, but it will also deter you from making impulse purchases that are not in your budget.

REACHING YOUR GOALS FASTER

If you want to reach your savings goals faster, you need to increase your income or decrease your expenses (or ideally a combination of both). This will give you more money to put towards your savings goals each month. Brainstorm ways to increase your income and reduce your expenses. An extra $100 a week from an additional income source can leave you with an extra $5200 a year in your savings account.

SAVING FOR A HOUSE

1. Research the market

2. Speak with a bank or mortgage broker

3. Be mindful of future costs of ownership

4. Calculate your deposit goal

5. Break down your goal

6. Make it a part of your budget and automate it

Buying a house to live in or as an investment is something many people aspire to do at some stage in their life. It can be a daunting process and is a significant financial decision that needs to be planned for in advance.

To figure out your savings goal, start off by determining how much you will need to save up as a deposit. A house deposit is typically 0 to 20 per cent of the property's purchase price (although it can also be anything above this amount). The deposit percentage will be agreed between you and the bank, depending on the value of the property, whether it is for an investment or for owner-occupier, your financial position (income, expenses, assets and liabilities), and the market conditions at the time you are taking out the loan.

Search for the specific areas, number of bedrooms and property land size that you have in mind, and determine an appropriate figure to use for your deposit-saving calculation. Doing this research will give you a greater understanding of what is realistic and feasible for you. It's also a good idea to chat to the bank or a mortgage broker about this, and they can give you an indication of the price range you can afford and the deposit amount that you will likely need to pay.

For example:

- Apartment value: $550 000

- Percentage deposit required: 15% (includes allowance for associated purchasing fees)

- Savings deposit required: $82 500*.

  * Numbers used are for illustrative purposes only.

Once you know how much you need to save up, break this down and make it a part of your monthly budget. If your goal is to save $40 000 for a deposit in three years, you will need to set aside approximately $1110 a month. Make this a part of your budget and set up an automatic transfer into your savings account every time you get paid so it happens without you needing to think or worry about it.

Be mindful of the additional purchasing fees when buying a property as well as the future expenses that will arise post-purchase. Not only will you have a mortgage expense (which may change over time depending on the loan type and interest rate changes), but also additional expenses for insurances, utility bills, taxes and maintenance. Before purchasing, create a 'future' budget that incorporates all of these expenses, and determine how this impacts the rest of your money management. These expenses may significantly influence the value and type of property you are able to purchase.

SAVING MONEY ON YOUR BILLS

| Set reminders | Cut down on non-essential expenses | Do your research | Negotiate |

Saving money on your bills is a great way to reduce your ongoing expenses without compromising on your wellbeing or living situation. There is no difference in the electricity that comes into our homes, so why not switch to the service provider with the best deal? Various service providers are in competition to acquire and retain you as a customer, so you can use this to your advantage to negotiate the best deal you can.

SET REMINDERS

Make a note or use the reminder app on your phone to keep track of how much you're currently paying for all your bills and when these bills are coming up for renewal or expiry. The best time to renegotiate your bills is at the time of renewal, so don't miss this opportunity. Things like insurance typically go up at the same time each year, so it's handy to set a reminder just before to evaluate your options and see if your policy is competitive.

CUT DOWN ON NON-ESSENTIAL EXPENSES

We often get so caught up in our day-to-day lives that we get to the point where we are just paying bills without taking a closer look at exactly what we are paying for. To review this, start off by auditing your regular payments and identifying any that are non-essential. This may include subscriptions, online services or memberships that you rarely or never use. Cancelling these will free up a lot more room in your monthly budget to be re-allocated to your financial goals.

Secondly, review all of your bills in further detail and confirm that you are using all of the components that you are paying for. For example, do you use all the data included in your phone bill or can you lower your plan to a cheaper one in line with your actual usage? Are you paying for a premium membership when you are only using the services that come with a lower membership tier? Is your insurance covering an asset that you no longer own? Taking a closer look at your coverage and adjusting accordingly can save you hundreds a month.

DO YOUR RESEARCH

Know what the market rate is for the bills you are paying and research competitors' offers. If you are a 'set and forget' type of bill payer, you may be missing out on existing offers that your current provider is promoting or an opportunity to switch to another provider who can provide the same service at a cheaper price. This research can also be used as leverage when you negotiate with your existing provider for a better rate.

NEGOTIATE

If your research has found that you are paying more money than you should be, it is time to negotiate a better deal. Call your provider and explain that you would like to remain as their customer but feel that they could be providing you with a better rate for their service based on other offers in the market (including their own). Negotiate a discount with them by being polite but firm.

While the best time to negotiate is when your service is up for renewal, don't hesitate to make the call as soon as you know there is a better rate out there. Be mindful of any cancellation or exit fees before making the switch. Saving a small percentage across all of your bills could be saving you thousands of dollars each year.

On the next page is a script that you can use when negotiating your bills.

Hi!

My name is [NAME] and I have been a loyal customer of [COMPANY] for [NUMBER OF YEARS] years.

I would like to remain a customer of yours, however, I have recently noticed that [COMPETITOR COMPANY A] and [COMPETITOR COMPANY B] are offering a better deal on the same [PRODUCT/SERVICE] you are providing.

[OUTLINE THE OFFER PROVIDED BY COMPETITORS]

Would you be able to price match or better these offers?

If they say no:

Can you offer me a loyalty discount or any other promotional rate?

If they still say no:

Consider changing your provider and lowering your monthly bills.

SAVING MONEY ON GROCERIES

✔ Plan your meals
✔ Make a list
✔ Shop online
✔ Explore alternatives
✔ Monitor specials/offers
✔ Sign up to rewards programs

The ever-increasing cost of groceries across the board has placed a serious strain on grocery budgets. Where $100 used to fill up your trolley, it may now barely get you through the week. It is also incredibly easy to overspend on groceries with all the different options and temptations that are placed in front of us. Buying groceries every week is unavoidable, but there are ways that you can stretch your money further and reduce your total bill.

PLAN YOUR MEALS

Spend some time each week planning your meals for the following week (this can include some takeaways that you've budgeted for). Meal prep on Sundays so you don't get tempted by expensive takeaway options during the week after a long day at work. Plan your meals around what produce is in season, as these items will typically be cheaper. Incorporate more meat-free meals into your week; reducing your meat intake will not only save you money, but there are numerous health and environmental benefits.

MAKE A LIST

Create a list of all the groceries you need so you don't aimlessly add to your trolley. Before you head to the shops, check your fridge and pantry to see what you already have so you aren't doubling up. If you are starting to over-fill your fridge and pantry, focus on using those groceries up before buying anything new.

SHOP ONLINE

Purchasing your groceries online means you won't be tempted to add random items as you stroll through the aisles. Online grocery ordering allows you to easily stick to your shopping list and see the weekly specials on offer. You will also be able to clearly see the total cost of your groceries before getting to the check-out, keeping yourself accountable for sticking to your grocery budget.

EXPLORE ALTERNATIVES

Exploring alternatives for the types of groceries you buy, as well as where you buy them from, is a great way to reduce your grocery bill without compromising on quality or taste. Opt for store-brand versions of common goods, and don't be afraid of frozen alternatives or using your freezer to extend the life of your groceries and avoid unnecessary waste. Another tip is to try to find products that are multi-purpose; for example, instead of having five different types of cleaning products, see if there is an all-in-one option that can save you money. Alternatively, check out your local markets or bulk food stores for discounts. Weekend farmers markets often have fresh produce at a much chapter price than supermarkets and bulk-buy stores are great to stock up on essentials, such as toilet paper and long-life items.

MONITOR SPECIALS/OFFERS

Monitor the specials and offers across all your local grocery stores each week. Keep an eye on deals for your favourite items and the essential groceries you are buying each week. Finding a great sale may be an opportunity to buy in bulk and save money for the coming weeks.

SIGN UP TO REWARDS PROGRAMS

Most major grocery stores have loyalty programs where you can earn rewards for your spend and/or receive exclusive discounts. Signing up to these programs is usually free and you earn points each time you do your grocery shop.

SAVING MONEY ON TRAVEL

Being conscious about your spending both before and during your trip can save you a lot of money. Saving money on your travel doesn't need to impact the quality of your trip or the experiences you are getting. Taking the time to research and plan your trip can save you hundreds of dollars that can be used instead as spending money.

PLANNING YOUR TRAVELS

- Set a budget for your trip. Determine how you will be getting around and if you will be staying in hotels, hostels, Airbnbs, camping or other arrangements. Set a realistic budget based on the locations and length of time that you will be travelling for.

- Sign up for airline newsletters and sales alerts to keep updated on upcoming sales.

- Be flexible with your travel dates. Avoiding school holidays and leaving mid-week instead of on weekends can be a lot cheaper.

- Try and book everything you can as far in advance as possible. Waiting too long to make bookings will only increase the cost of your travel.

- Book directly with the hotel. Often this will be cheaper as third-party websites add an extra commission fee.

- Before you book, search for discount codes or cashback offers to see if you can save on your flights and accommodation.

DURING YOUR TRAVELS

- Ask locals for their recommendations of restaurants and street markets. Avoid eating in the main tourist areas as their prices are usually inflated.

- Shop at the local grocery stores and pack snacks and water for the day of exploring or cook dinner some nights.

- Use a credit/debit card with no foreign transaction fees. These fees will add up quickly.

- Get a local SIM card with internet data for your phone. This is usually much cheaper than paying for international roaming charges.

- Pack food and water for the airport and other transits. If you have an empty water bottle, take this through the airport security and fill it up at your gate to save money and help the environment.

- Research free attractions and activities at the place you are going to. Many places have free nights during the week and local events.

- If you are planning on visiting a lot of attractions, get a city attraction card to save money on all the admission fees.

4

Spending money

HOW TO SHOP SMARTER

- Question yourself

- Calculate the hours of work required

- Determine cost per wear/use

- Consider renting, borrowing or buying second-hand

- Look for a discount code or cashback

Shopping is both a necessity and a weakness for many of us. We are constantly inundated with advertisements from our favourite brands and new products trying to grab our attention that it can be easy to splurge and go over budget. It is, therefore, important to make smarter shopping decisions so that the money you do spend is worthwhile. Seeking value for money is not about finding the cheapest options. It is about finding the best option for what you need. This may be choosing to hire a dress instead of buying it, opting for a higher quality version of an item so it lasts longer or questioning whether you need to buy the item in the first place.

QUESTION YOURSELF

Before you buy something, ask yourself the following questions:

- Is it a want or a need?
- Does it align with your financial goals and values?
- Is it within your budget?
- Do you have something similar already?
- Do you have space for it?
- Is it worth the price?
- Is it high quality?

Reflect on your answers to each question and assess whether the purchase is still necessary or worthwhile.

CALCULATE HOURS OF WORK

A super effective strategy to help you decide whether you truly need something is the hours of work calculation. Instead of asking how much something costs, ask yourself how many hours of work you need to work to pay for it.

Converting the purchase price of the item puts the value of the item into the context of your time, a resource that is seen as much more valuable than money itself. Looking at the item through this perspective can make us realise that we don't really need the object as there may be something else to spend our money (and time) on.

For example: Let's say, after tax, you make $20 an hour.

- An $80 bag would cost you four hours of work.
- A $200 pair of sneakers would cost you 10 hours of work.
- A $2500 designer bag would cost you 125 hours of work.

4	**10**	**125 hours**
hours	hours	of work
of work	of work	

Once you have determined how many hours you need to work, assess whether you are willing to work that many hours to buy the item.

DETERMINE COST PER WEAR/USE

Another strategy that can help you make smarter purchases is calculating the cost per wear/use. Considering the cost per wear/use of an item pushes you to think about how many times this item will be worn or used to then determine if it is a value-for-money decision to purchase it. Using this perspective will lead you to make more high-quality, thoughtful purchases and reduce your environmental impact.

To calculate the cost per wear/use of an item, you divide the cost of the item by the number of times you anticipate that you will wear or use it. For example, if you are looking to purchase a new dress for a wedding that costs $500, but you know you will never wear it again, the cost per wear of that item is $500. Whereas a $500 classic black dress that is more versatile and can be worn 15 times a year has a cost per wear of $33. This highlights that the classic black dress is a much better value-for-money purchase.

RENT, BORROW OR BUY SECOND-HAND

Instead of buying something new, explore whether you can rent, borrow or buy it second-hand. This is not only a cost-effective option, but it is a far more sustainable one. Before making a purchase, consider whether you can get it second-hand. Check Facebook Marketplace, eBay and buy/swap/sell groups on Facebook where you can get the item in great condition for a fraction of the price. For items that you only need to use for a once-off occasion, consider renting through a hire site or borrowing from a friend or family member. You will be able to save a lot of money by hiring that expensive dress, textbook or home renovation tool.

LOOK FOR A DISCOUNT CODE/CASHBACK

Before making any purchase online, check to see if you can find a discount code or cashback offer. Online stores are running sales almost all year, so the chances of finding a current discount code is quite high. Head to their website and look for an email sign-up bonus discount, search through Google or use a coupon-finding browser extension to find a working coupon. There is also a range of cashback platforms you can utilise to earn money back on all your purchases.

COMMUNITY STORY
A spending challenge

A few years ago I discovered op-shopping, which I soon became obsessed with. Decent quality clothes for cheap? My teenage self was astounded! I saw this as an opportunity to minimise my spending on basics and find cool/different clothes for an affordable price.

Eventually, I had too many clothes in my cupboard, and it was becoming increasingly difficult to find space to fit new items. I gave away clothes I had never worn, but I was still buying more clothes, usually second hand. Despite knowing I was reducing waste by giving new life to second-hand clothing, I eventually realised that if I was not wearing both the old and new clothes, I was contributing to the problem. Plus, I was spending money on items that I simply did not need.

I concluded that, to reduce waste and my spending habits, I had to set a challenge for myself to not buy any clothes for an entire year.

The idea was a little extreme, and I also had to account for work clothes, so I decided I would allow myself 12 items of clothing for the year — one for each month — as at the time I received a monthly clothing allowance for my job. I did not want to fail my own challenge, so I increased my limit to 15 items of clothing in case I found something I desperately liked or needed to replace a staple piece.

By sharing this challenge on my Instagram story, with friends and customers at work, it has helped keep me accountable. Some factors did change a couple of things, such as a spontaneous overseas trip and starting a new job, where I received another clothing allowance, but I have been adamant in my decision to reduce fashion waste in my own home and be disciplined with my spending habits.

This goal has significantly changed the way that I make financial decisions. I now consider the versatility of the item/service I'm looking into, the amount of use I will get out of it, how I can use it to benefit myself and others, and how I can invest my money into something that will potentially minimise my spending in the long term.

Izzy

STOP IMPULSE SHOPPING

Be aware of your mood

Create a needs list

Wait before you buy

Ignore marketing tactics

STOP

You've had a bad day at work and you arrive home exhausted, frustrated and defeated. You open up your laptop and start scrolling through the website of your favourite online store. Buying something new will boost your mood, right? You impulsively hit buy and your brain releases a temporary hit of dopamine that makes you feel good.

An impulse purchase is anything you buy that was unplanned or unaccounted for within your budget. It can be anything from a chocolate bar at the check-out line of the supermarket or a larger purchase, like a new designer handbag or car. There are several reasons why we impulse shop, including our feelings and emotions, finding a 'too good to be true' sale or deal and poor money management.

The issue with impulse shopping is that it often leads to overspending. Your budget can and should allocate money to spend on yourself. Going over this budget with impulse purchases made on a whim may result in you having to take money out of your savings or use credit to purchase the items.

BE AWARE OF YOUR MOOD

Our purchasing habits can often be influenced by our emotions. Emotional spending habits subconsciously make you spend money to magnify or replace an emotion, whether that emotion is good or bad. The result of these emotional spending habits is usually an unplanned, impulse purchase that is often regretted later. Some things that may lead you to impulse shop include boredom, the fear of missing out on an item or sale, stress/burnout, the desire to feel worthy, peer pressure, feeling anxious before a social event, trying to 'keep up' with other people or the latest trend, sadness, convincing yourself that something is a 'need' or having a 'you only live once' mindset. Being able to identify your emotional spending habits is the first step to helping you overcome impulse spending.

WAIT BEFORE YOU BUY

If you have the urge to spend, wait 24 to 48 hours. After this time period has elapsed, consider whether you still want to make the purchase. Most of the time, you'll realise you never wanted or needed the item in the first place.

CREATE A NEEDS LIST

Keep a note on your phone of all the items you need to buy. This could be anything from groceries to skincare top-ups or new boots for winter to replace your ones that have worn out. When you are about to purchase an item, check your list. If the item is not on there, don't buy it.

IGNORE MARKETING TACTICS

We are constantly bombarded with new products, flash sales and marketing information from our favourite brands through emails, social media and across the internet. Avoid the temptation of buying things you do not need by unsubscribing from the email lists and unfollowing your favourite brands and stores online. Further, do not feel pressured to buy an item because the sale is ending soon. Retailers have been using this 'fear of missing out' marketing tactic to boost sales for years. There will always be another sale or discount on the item.

COMMUNITY STORY

Reversing bad spending habits

I used to spend money frivolously. The more money I made, the more I spent. I worked hard, so I simply shopped hard, and I didn't see a problem with it until I had an insane amount of credit card debt and no real assets to my name. Have you seen the movie *Confessions of a Shopaholic*? Yep, I found myself relating to that narrative. I knew I needed to process what finance meant to me in relation to being in a financially stable place, and reverse the bad habits, pay off the debt and build my portfolio. After years of poor management, I finally started reading advice from finance bloggers and learned from others on Instagram. I came across Smart Women Society and have recently started organising my goals with their Ultimate Money Makeover Game Plan bundle.

My biggest money tip: It takes time! It takes time to change habits, but with a solid savings plan and measurable goals, you can become better at money management — it is possible! Stay consistent in the specific areas of finance you are targeting. Also, read. Read about finance and learn, because the more you learn, the more you understand how important it is to be a good manager of your money!

Allie

NAVIGATING MONEY WITH FRIENDS

Navigating money with your friends can be challenging due to the diverse situations we are all in. We have all been through different life experiences, and have varying incomes and individual values that affect our relationships with money. Money should not be a contentious point in your friendship. There should be no pressure to 'keep up' with each other or constantly compare your circumstances to your friends. People with strong friendships respect each other's unique circumstances, openly discuss their financial goals and support each other to achieve these goals. Creating a safe space for everyone to share their financial journey and voice when something is not in their budget is key.

Discuss your financial goals together

Be each other's accountability partner

Suggest budget-friendly catch-ups

Avoid comparison/ trying to 'keep up'

Share financial knowledge and tools

Be respectful and understand that everyone's situation is unique

Be open when something isn't in your budget

DISCUSS YOUR FINANCIAL GOALS TOGETHER

We love to discuss our weekend adventures, work frustrations and dating lives with our friends, but more often than not we tend to shy away from discussing any money-related topics. Sharing your financial goals with your friends can not only keep you motivated along your journey, but it will also keep you accountable to put in the work to achieve them. By sharing your goals, you will also naturally discuss experiences that have gone well as well as the challenges you have faced so you can all learn and grow from each other.

SUGGEST BUDGET-FRIENDLY CATCH-UPS

You and your friends should respect each other's financial position and money goals, and create a judgement-free environment when it comes to money. By doing so, everyone will feel comfortable with openly stating that they don't want to participate in an activity that is currently out of their budget. This does not mean that you or your friend values saving more than the friendship, but it creates mutual respect for each other's financial goals and journeys. If you are working hard towards a particular goal, or if you know that a friend is doing the same, suggest budget-friendly alternatives when catching up, such as going on a walk, grabbing a coffee, visiting your local art gallery or hanging out at each other's homes. You will have just as much fun having a dinner party at your house as going out to an expensive restaurant.

AVOID COMPARISON/TRYING TO 'KEEP UP'

It is highly unlikely that all your friends share the same identical income and expenses as you. We all pursue different career paths and have varying priorities and attitudes towards how we spend our money. Trying to keep up or comparing yourself financially to your friends can be detrimental to your financial position and cause issues with your friendship.

It's natural to feel a bit jealous or down when your friend hits a huge financial milestone that you have not yet achieved. Maybe it's a big job promotion or they've just bought their first house. Try and re-frame your perspective in these situations. Clap for your friend, genuinely celebrate their achievement and take it as inspiration and motivation for what you too can accomplish. On a similar note, you do not need to overspend or spend beyond your means to keep up with what your friends are doing. A true friend will never pressure you or make you feel bad for not having the same things as them.

It is not a race. There is no competition. The only person you should be comparing yourself to is yourself. As long as you are doing better than you were a day, a month or a year ago, you are doing an amazing job.

BE EACH OTHER'S ACCOUNTABILITY PARTNER

The best financial friend is one who keeps you accountable and supports you on your financial journey. Cheer each other on and regularly remind each other of how you will feel when you finally achieve your goals. Brainstorm new ideas to increase your income or decrease your expenses to reach your goals faster. As we discussed in chapter 1, achieving a financial goal is not a linear process. There will be ups and downs and you will lose momentum. When this does happen, support your friend and encourage them to get back on track and try again.

BE RESPECTFUL AND UNDERSTANDING THAT EVERYONE'S SITUATION IS UNIQUE

We are all at different stages of our money journey. We all come from different upbringings, privileges and backgrounds and have varying incomes, priorities and circumstances that impact our financial position. Always be kind, respectful and understanding that everyone's situation is unique and support your friends in reaching their individual goals.

BE OPEN WHEN SOMETHING ISN'T IN YOUR BUDGET

Catching up with friends does not have to be expensive and you should be comfortable letting them know when something is not in your budget. Below are some phrases you can try next time a friend suggests doing something out of budget.

- 'I'm working really hard on [financial goal]; can we do [cheaper alternative] instead?'
- 'I would love to go out for dinner, but I haven't budgeted for it this month. Did you want to come over to my house instead?'
- 'I would love to catch up. Let's grab a coffee!'
- 'I've heard amazing things about [cheaper restaurant/bar], how about we try there?'
- 'Are you free this weekend? There's a new exhibit at the art gallery I think you would enjoy.'

SHARE FINANCIAL KNOWLEDGE AND TOOLS

Your friends are not your competition. Openly share and discuss any financial knowledge and tools that you discover or learn about. If you find a shopping hack, a budgeting tool that you love or a great financial resource, let them know. We are so much stronger together so it is important to lift each other up so we can all succeed in our financial journeys.

5

Growing your money

TYPES OF INCOME

1. Earned income

2. Profit income

3. Interest income

4. Dividend income

5. Rental income

6. Royalty income

7. Capital gains income

At the end of the day, there is only so much you can cut down your expenses by, and there will be a point in your money journey where reducing your expenses no longer becomes realistic. Once you are in control of your expenses, it's time to increase your income. Increasing your income and creating new income streams, while also maintaining your current level of spending, is the true key to developing your wealth. Let's explore the seven different types of income.

1. EARNED INCOME

Your earned income is the money you receive from working a job for a salary or wage. The first step for anyone looking to increase their income is reviewing their pay with their employer. Are you due for a pay rise? When is the next round of promotions? What is the market rate for the job you do? If your current employer is not receptive to a pay increase, you may need to look elsewhere. Use an online job-search website to research other similar jobs in your city, and review how the remuneration compares to your current salary/wage. The information in chapter 6 can help you with this process. A 10 to 20 per cent increase in your salary or wage can make a huge difference in relieving financial stress and reaching your goals faster.

2. PROFIT INCOME

Profit income refers to selling products or services for more than they cost to earn a profit. Typically this income is earned by starting a business or a side hustle. For example, if you sell paintings for $300 and the materials and your labour cost $200, your profit on the sale is $100.

3. INTEREST INCOME

Receiving interest income from lending your money can be in the form of a bank savings account, personal loaning to others, term deposits or bonds. For example, if you have money in a high-interest savings account, the bank will pay you a percentage of your balance as interest. The interest you receive is usually expressed as a percentage per annum and the exact percentage amount will vary between different account types.

4. DIVIDEND INCOME

Dividend income is money you earn from owning shares in a company. The company shares a portion of their profits with shareholders in the form of a dividend. It is important to note that not every company pays out dividends.

5. RENTAL INCOME

Renting your assets to others can be a profitable way to make additional income. While we typically think rental income only relates to real estate, there is also opportunity to rent other assets that you own such as cars, boats, bikes, clothing and gardening tools.

6. ROYALTY INCOME

Royalty income can be earned by allowing someone to use something you have designed, built or made in return for a percentage rate or fixed payment amount. For example, a musician can receive royalty payments when their song is streamed, played on radio or used in an advertisement. An engineer could patent the design of a new piece of technology and receive royalties from a company utilising this idea to develop a product.

7. CAPITAL GAINS INCOME

Capital gains income refers to profit earned on the sale of an asset that has increased in value since you bought it. This may be from a property value increase, increase in company ownership value or other intangible assets such as shares. While the capital gain can be leveraged prior to selling the asset, the capital gain income is only realised income once the asset is sold.

WHY YOU SHOULD INVEST

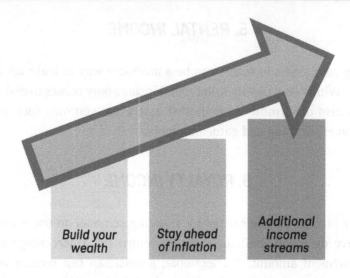

Build your
wealth

Stay ahead
of inflation

Additional
income
streams

Once you've mastered your money management, it's time to start putting your money to work. There are no shortcuts to growing your wealth and reaching financial independence. You need to understand the opportunities that exist, and which ones best suit your needs now and into the future. The key to achieving financial independence is investing as soon as possible and as consistently as possible to capitalise on compounding growth. There are a variety of investment options you can explore, such as shares, property and superannuation. Make sure to do your research, understand the risks involved and talk to a professional for assistance on your personal situation.

BUILD YOUR WEALTH

Investing has the potential to help you grow your wealth. The sooner you start investing, the more you can take advantage of the benefits time has on compounding growth. The benefit of time in investing is based on the concept of compound interest. Compound interest refers to earning interest on interest, and causes your money to compound and grow exponentially over time.

To explain the concept simply, let's say you invest $1000, which earns a 10 per cent return each year (with no regular contributions).

- After the first year, you will earn $100 in interest (10 per cent of $1000), and the total investment value becomes $1100.

- After the second year, you earn $110 in interest (10 per cent of $1100), and the total investment value becomes $1210 and so on.

If you also added regular deposits of $100 per month into the above scenario, after a 40-year period, the investment will be worth approximately $576 000 from a contribution of only $48 000 (based on a consistent 10 per cent growth rate, compounded annually).

While it is hard to see the progression over a short period of time, accumulating compound interest over a longer period results in some significant money growth. The most important thing is to get started. The best day to start investing was yesterday, the second-best day is today.

STAY AHEAD OF INFLATION

You may have heard the saying that 'inflation is the silent killer of wealth'. But what does that actually mean? To take a step back, inflation is the rate at which prices increase over time. Every country around the world has a different inflation rate, with many having positive inflation rates year on year (i.e. prices are increasing every year). As prices increase, it results in you being able to buy less than you could last year with the same amount of money. Your money, therefore, becomes less valuable each year. Investing your money allows you to grow your money to keep up with the increasing prices of goods and services.

ADDITIONAL INCOME STREAM

Investing may also provide an additional income stream. If you invest in property, this income would be from the rent that you receive. If you invest in shares, this income would be from dividends received. When a company makes a profit, they may decide to distribute some of it to its shareholders as profit. You can receive this money as cash or set up an automatic reinvestment plan. There are no guarantees of additional income through investing. You should review the risks involved and speak to a professional for personal advice to determine what is the best option for you.

BEFORE YOU START INVESTING

Build an
emergency
fund

Pay off
high-interest
debts

Know your
cashflow
and goals

Do your
research

All investing involves risk. This risk refers to the likelihood that you will lose some or all of the money you have invested due to your investment falling in value or not performing as well as expected. The key to successful investing is planning ahead and being informed. Before you start investing, you need to make sure you have a good handle on your budget and cashflow, understand your goals and risk tolerance, and research and understand key investing concepts. You can then create a plan of how much you want to invest and what you want to invest in.

BUILD UP AN EMERGENCY FUND

Make sure you have built up an adequate emergency fund (see chapter 2 for more on this) to cover three to six months of your essential expenses. While you may have money in your investments, not all investments are liquid or easily accessible. Having an emergency fund built up will ensure you won't run into any trouble or have to sell long-term investments if unexpected emergencies arise.

KNOW YOUR CASHFLOW AND GOALS

Understanding your budget (see chapter 2) and cashflow helps you determine how much surplus money you have to put into investments. A budget will show you how much income you make each month, your expenses and the funds you have available to put towards your financial goals. Knowing your short-, medium- and long-term financial goals is also important. Investing is a long-term strategy, so if you are wanting to travel, have a wedding or buy a house in the next few years, you should be keeping money for these in savings accounts instead of high-risk investments.

PAY OFF HIGH-INTEREST DEBTS

High-interest debt, such as credit cards and personal loans, hinders your ability to grow your wealth and achieve financial independence. Grab a sheet of paper and write down all your debts, their current balances, the minimum repayment and the interest rate. Determine your debt pay-off strategy (the two most popular strategies are the debt avalanche and the debt snowball methods; see chapter 2 for more on this) and put as much money as possible towards paying down your high-interest debts. Once you have paid off high-interest debt, you will free up your cash flow and you can re-allocate this money towards your investments.

DO YOUR RESEARCH

Don't go into investing without understanding your risk tolerance, the different investing asset classes, and the potential risks and returns they possess. Research concepts such as volatility and diversification, so you understand how to reduce your portfolio's risk by spreading your money across and within asset classes. You should also look into the different avenues/platforms you may be able to invest through and the tax implications on earnings from your investments.

TYPES OF INVESTMENTS

The best investment is the one that is aligned with your financial goals, your appetite for risk and the time period that you want to invest in. To know what investment to choose, it is important to understand the various types of investments.

TYPES OF ASSETS

The types of assets you can invest in can be split into defensive and growth investments.

DEFENSIVE INVESTMENTS

Defensive investments are generally predictable and, therefore, offer a lower risk option for investors. They aim to provide stable returns and portfolio diversification to protect the capital that has been invested. Typically, defensive investments are made to meet short-term financial goals in the next three years.

Defensive investments include:

- Cash: such as bank accounts, high-interest savings accounts and term deposits. Cash is the most liquid and secure asset, useful for short-term savings and your emergency fund. It has the lowest risk, but also the lowest return.

- Fixed interest: such as corporate bonds, government bonds and capital notes. Investing in a bond means you are lending money to the government or a company, and they pay you interest at regular intervals in return. This type of asset offers consistent returns over a specified period of time and is relatively secure if you lend to the government or financially stable companies.

Defensive investments vs growth investments

DEFENSIVE INVESTMENTS

Cash

Fixed interest

GROWTH INVESTMENTS

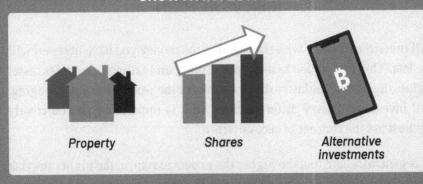

Property

Shares

Alternative investments

GROWTH INVESTMENTS

Growth investments are generally more uncertain investments, but they offer a higher potential return when compared with defensive investments. The rates of return and capital growth of these investments are volatile. Typically growth investments are made to meet longer-term financial goals of more than three years.

Growth investments include:

- Shares: such as stocks This type of asset represents ownership/ equity in a company. It is highly liquid and can offer capital growth as well as dividend income.

- Real estate: such as investing in residential or commercial property. This asset type can earn you a steady stream of rental income and offer capital growth over time; however, this asset type is not liquid and can incur significant expenses to maintain the asset.

- Alternative investments: such as private equity, commodities and cryptocurrency. Returns differ across these investment types but they all aim for capital growth.

RISK VS RETURN

All investments come with the risk that the money you have invested will be lost. This can be due to underperforming and failing companies, asset values decreasing, industry developments or the world economy changing. All investments carry different risks, so it is important that you clearly understand the concept of risk vs return.

It is generally said that the higher the expected return, the higher the risk of the investment. Similarly, the lower the expected return, the lower the risk. Defensive assets are lower risk, whereas growth assets are higher risk and more volatile. This is not always the case, and past returns should not be an indication of future returns when you are choosing your investment.

When deciding on an investment, ask yourself:

- How would I feel if I lost all of this investment?
- What would the impact of losing all of this investment be?
- Is this risk worth the potential return?

DIVERSIFICATION

Diversification refers to spreading your investments across and within asset classes to reduce your portfolio's volatility and risk over time. Through diversification, your risk portfolio lowers based on the idea that in different economic periods some asset classes will fall while others will increase. This strategy is the most effective way to safeguard your portfolio against a single investment failing or performing badly. To determine your current diversification, list out all of your investments and their value. This will highlight if your portfolio is heavily weighted towards one asset class, and whether you should diversify more or rebalance your portfolio.

DECIDING WHAT TO INVEST IN

When making your decision about what to invest in, make sure you understand and are able to confidently answer the following questions:

- How does this investment work?
- What is the expected return on the investment? Will it be capital growth, income or both?
- What are the risks involved with this investment?
- Are there any fees and charges associated with buying, selling or holding the investment?
- What is the process of selling the investment? How long does it take to convert the investment into cash?
- Are there any tax or legal implications of the investment?

- Does the investment contribute to a diversified portfolio?
- Does the investment align with my ethics and values?
- Have you read the product disclosure statement (PDS) to understand exactly what the investment includes?
- If the investment fails, what is the impact on your overall finances and life?

Remember, if you are not comfortable with making an investment decision or need personalised advice, speak with a finance professional.

CAREER

In this section:

If there is one thing you get out of this book and apply to your career (or any aspect of your life), let it be this: *Shoot your shot.*

The best things that have ever happened to me in my career happened because I took a risk.

- A spur-of-the-moment pitch mid-meal to the owner of a new local restaurant landed me my first client for my social media marketing side hustle.

- Applying for a job that I was not 100 per cent qualified for scored me one of the most rewarding roles I have ever worked in.

- Negotiating my salary led to a 30 per cent pay increase and money that would have otherwise been left on the table.

- Putting my hand up for a new project led me to meeting the most inspiring career mentor.

- A random DM on Instagram led to a national diary collaboration with one of the biggest diary manufacturers in the country.

None of these would have ever happened if I didn't shoot my shot.

How many times have you talked yourself out of a potential opportunity because you didn't feel worthy or experienced or qualified enough? But if you never go for what you want, you'll never have it. If you never push yourself out of your comfort zone, you'll never grow. If you don't ask, the answer will always be 'no'.

Imagine how much you could achieve if you weren't afraid of failure or other people's opinions or feeling embarrassed. Stop creating roadblocks for yourself. Your potential is infinite. Feel that fear and hesitation and do it anyway. Write that email. Send that message. Make that phone call. Ask that question. Don't sit and wait for opportunities to come your way. Take charge and create them for yourself.

If you feel any self-doubt or self-sabotaging thoughts creep in, challenge them.

So what if they say no?

So what if it doesn't work out this one time?

So what if you make mistakes and learn along the way?

Shooting your shot isn't always easy. It will be scary, nerve-wracking and uncomfortable. But don't let the temporary discomfort override the possibility of a life-changing win. You might fail the first time or even the tenth time, but that 11th attempt will make it all worth it. Reframe failure as redirection and trust that you are on the path to exactly what is meant for you. Keep backing yourself, no matter how many tries it takes.

6

Getting
a job

COMPONENTS OF A
WINNING RESUMÉ

1. Max two pages

2. Simple and easy-to-read design

3. Tailored for the specific job you are applying for

4. Lists accomplishments and includes your 'it' factor

5. Includes quantitative details

1. MAX TWO PAGES

A recruiter spends on average seven to ten seconds looking at your resumé. Keep it between one and two pages max. If you have a lot of experience, prioritise the experience that is most relevant to the job you are applying for. You do not need to include your first part-time job at the local store when you were 15.

2. SIMPLE AND EASY-TO-READ DESIGN

Your resumé should be simple and organised so the recruiter can quickly skim over it and see that you have the appropriate skills and experience for the job. On the next page is an example of a simple resumé design that you can use. You can reorder any of these elements depending on what you want to highlight, your experience level, age and priorities.

The appropriate design for your resumé will depend on the industry and company you are applying for. If you are applying for a role in a creative industry or a start-up, you may choose to have a more aesthetically pleasing style for your resumé. On the other hand, a more traditional, black-and-white resumé may be better suited to corporate positions.

Many companies nowadays also use applicant tracking system (ATS) software to filter through applications in the early stages of the recruitment process. The software compares the text in your application and resumé against the job description to check if it meets certain pre-determined criteria (e.g., that you have a bachelor's degree). Regardless of the industry you are applying for, make sure the formatting and design of your resumé is clear and easy to read to avoid being rejected by the ATS software.

3. TAILORED FOR THE SPECIFIC JOB YOU ARE APPLYING FOR

It is painfully clear to a recruiter when you have submitted the same generic resumé you have had saved on your desktop for years. Tailoring your resumé for the specific job you are applying for not only shows that you have taken the time to understand the intricacies of the job description, but it also positions you as the best candidate for the role.

You may be groaning right now at the thought of writing a completely new resumé every time you apply for a job, but there's no need to. Create a base resumé template and spend a few minutes tweaking this where necessary

Your simple resumé design

First and Last Name

State your title and industry (or top skills if changing careers).

CONTACT

- Email address
- Phone number
- Links to your LinkedIn profile and/or portfolio (if relevant)

EDUCATION

- Include name of the school and any majors
- If new graduate or early career, can include activities/clubs and high school

SKILLS

- Technical skills, language proficiencies, certifications, awards, personal interests

INTRODUCTION (optional)

- Also referred to as a resumé objective, summary of experience or branding statement
- This is optional, but if you do include it, keep it brief (max. 1-2 sentences)

WORK/PROFESSIONAL EXPERIENCE

- The most important part of your resumé
- Include 2-5 of your most relevant and major work experiences
- Specify the company, location, job title and length of time worked in that position
- Use bullet points and action verbs to take credit for your work
- Show your impact and results using numbers and quantitative achievements

NOTE: You do not need to include your references on your resumé. If the company would like to get in contact with your references, they will ask for their details.

for each new application. Here are three easy steps to follow to tweak your resumé in less than five minutes.

1. Review the job description carefully and make a list of all the key skills, responsibilities and requirements.

2. Based on that list, remove or reorder any components of your resumé to highlight the relevant skills and experiences you have.

3. Add specific keywords from the job description throughout your resumé.

4. LISTS ACCOMPLISHMENTS AND INCLUDES YOUR 'IT FACTOR'

The work experience section of your resumé should contain clear and concise dot points listing all your accomplishments in previous roles. They should not be a reiteration of your job description or duties. Don't forget to call out your 'it' factor (i.e. things that would make you stand out from your competition). Have you worked on an identical project to the one you will be starting on in the new job? Have you worked with a key client before? Can you speak multiple languages? Whatever it is, make sure to clearly emphasise this in your resumé.

5. INCLUDES QUANTITATIVE DETAILS

What is the secret ingredient to making a good resumé a winning resumé?

Numbers.

Quantify results and achievements wherever possible in your resumé. For example, instead of saying, 'Grew the Instagram account', try 'Generated 250 per cent growth in the Instagram account'. See how much stronger that sounds?

Go through each line of your resumé and see where you can add quantitative results to support your points and take credit for your hard work. Some examples of your impact/results that you can quantify include:

- **Costs saved or money generated:** Did you reduce costs? Increase revenue? Acquire new clients?

- **Time saved:** Did you streamline a process? Improve response times?

- **Problems solved:** Did you resolve complaints? Reduce a common problem?

- **People helped:** Did you help colleagues or clients? Can you share your customer satisfaction score?

- **Recognition/awards received:** What were the metrics or reasons why you were given these awards?

Use the numerical form of the number (i.e. 3) instead of writing the word out (i.e. three) for greater impact. If you don't know the exact numbers, give your best estimate or a range.

COVER LETTERS

Ugh, cover letters. Also universally known as the worst part of the job application. The purpose of a cover letter is to attract or encourage the recruiter to read your resumé. A good cover letter is short and sweet (approximately 2 to 4 paragraphs), showcases your enthusiasm for applying for the role and explains why you are the best candidate. Similar to your resumé, you should tailor your cover letter every time you apply for a position and match the formality with the tone in the job description, the industry and the culture of the company you are applying for. If you're not sure, lean towards being more formal.

Who to address your cover letter to

Address your cover letter to the hiring manager/recruiter. If you can't find their name, address it to the team as a whole.

Paragraph 1: Introduce yourself

Explain who you are and emphasise your excitement and motivation for applying for the role.

Paragraph 2: Why you?

Highlight your relevant skills and experience that will make you successful in the role.

Paragraph 3: Why the company?

Do some research and explain why you want to work at this specific company.

Paragraph 4: Conclusion

Thank them for their consideration and re-confirm your enthusiasm in the role.

COMMUNITY STORY
A rocky road to success

I had a lot of difficulties finding a job after graduating from my undergrad degree. My classmates were landing dream roles right after graduation and although I was getting some interviews, nothing ever eventuated. I was looking at their successes and compared myself to their stage of life. I think it was 6 months post grad still no job, when I decided to just use the 'spray and pray' technique and literally scatter my resumé to ANY entry level job I saw online. I was desperate, and one start-up company did come back to me, so I accepted.

Ten months in, the start-up company I worked at hit REALLY hard times, and that resulted in me not being paid for six weeks. I think I was naive and trusted the founder too much, with her empty promises of, 'You're getting paid next week I promise!' I used ALL of my emergency funds in order to pay bills, which were already on final notice. The start-up ended up entering liquidation, and even with Fair Work helping me recoup the unpaid wages, the case went on for 1.5 years until I saw a single cent.

I was able to get a junior e-commerce role for a small family business quite soon after the start-up liquidated. I always yearned for more in this role, but my ideas for new campaigns and processes were always turned down. My confidence was at an all-time low, and it showed.

I turned on the 'actively looking' status on my LinkedIn when I was having a bad day at work one day. Suddenly, I was being propositioned for roles DOUBLE the salary I was on, and I just didn't get why. Looking back now, this was definitely the imposter syndrome kicking in. I don't know how, but one day I just woke up and said, 'F**k it, I have financial goals, and I am not going to kick them by thinking I'm not good enough!' And you know what? Turns out, it was all in my head, and once I cleaned up my resumé and practised interview questions, I had recruiters helping me negotiate insane salary packages at several companies that I never dreamt of being 'good enough' for.

Since then, I have changed jobs twice, but each time I have been able to negotiate better remuneration. I'm now, quite possibly, in my dream job. In June this year I bought my first apartment. Don't settle for less, know your worth and know that you CAN get it!

Danielle

ACING THE JOB INTERVIEW

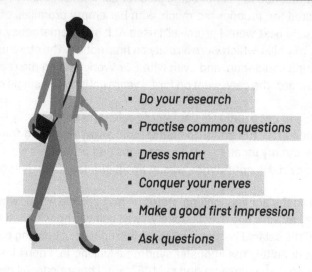

- Do your research
- Practise common questions
- Dress smart
- Conquer your nerves
- Make a good first impression
- Ask questions

You wowed the recruiter with your job application and you get a call to come for a job interview. Before you start panicking, remember that if you have reached the interview stage, the company already thinks you have what it takes to do the job. The interview is an opportunity for both you and the hiring manager to get to know each other better and see if there is a good fit for the role.

DO YOUR RESEARCH

Preparation is the key to acing your interview and securing the job. Start by conducting thorough background research about the company, the culture, the role and the interviewer(s). Familiarise yourself with the company's website and social media pages, search for any recent news articles and speak to any friends or connections that work/have worked at the company to gain their insights.

Understand the company history, mission, their products/services, key leaders, recent achievements, future plans and any involvement in industry events or community initiatives. Re-read the job description to remind yourself of the key responsibilities and where the position sits within the team and the wider organisation.

Before your interview, ask the HR manager or recruiter who will be interviewing you. Make sure you know their job title and how to pronounce their name. Look up the interviewer(s) on LinkedIn to learn more about them. This will help you see if you have anything in common, which you can then bring up during the interview to build rapport. You might be wondering 'Won't they think I'm creepy for stalking them?' While LinkedIn does notify a person when you have viewed their profile, most hiring managers will be impressed that you have done your research.

PRACTISE COMMON QUESTIONS

There are a variety of standard interview questions that are asked by most interviewers, regardless of the industry or level of seniority. Prepare responses for and practise answering these questions ahead of time so you aren't caught off guard during your interview. One of the most common types of questions are behavioural questions (i.e. questions that start with 'Tell me about a time when ... '). These questions are designed to uncover how you would respond in certain scenarios. Use the STAR (situation, task, action, result) technique to answer behavioural questions, providing a specific instance of how you handled or resolved a certain circumstance. Before going to your interview, brainstorm a list of stories or past experiences you have encountered that exemplify a variety of behaviours and adapt these to the specific questions that you are asked.

DRESS SMART

What you should wear to an interview will depend largely on the industry and the individual company's dress code. The best way to figure this out is to take a look at the company's website to see what their staff wear or ask the recruiter/HR manager what the appropriate dress code is. If you're still unsure, it is always better to be slightly overdressed than underdressed. Make sure your outfit is clean, ironed and fits well and keep your hair and makeup simple. Don't forget to pack a notepad, pen, copies of your resumé and the job description, as well as any work samples (if necessary). You can also bring in your research notes and a list of questions, but be careful not to rely on these during the interview.

CONQUER YOUR NERVES

It's completely normal to feel nervous before your job interview. Preparing and re-framing your mindset towards the interview will drastically boost your confidence on the day. In addition to your research and practice questions from page 97, be clear on the location and time of your interview. If the interview is in person, plan how you will get there and factor in traffic and parking. Aim to arrive 15 to 30 minutes early so you can familiarise yourself with where you need to go and do a final read over your notes. Reframe the interview as a two-way conversation. You are also interviewing the company to see whether it is a good fit for you and your career goals.

MAKE A GOOD FIRST IMPRESSION

Creating a great first impression and building rapport with the interviewer is key. They usually know within the first few minutes of the interview whether they want to hire you.

Smile and be polite to every person you interact with. Whether it's the receptionist or another team member, this can have a significant impact on the result of your interview. Sit up straight and make eye contact to show that you are engaged in the conversation. Take your time answering questions and if you feel overwhelmed or can't think of an answer, take a deep breath and gather your thoughts.

Avoid speaking poorly about your existing/previous employer, boss or co-worker and, instead, solely focus on why this opportunity is your next best step. Write down any important details or interesting conversation topics that you want to remember or mention in your thank you email. Don't forget to also ask your interviewer for their email address at the end of the interview if you don't already have it.

QUESTIONS TO ASK AT THE END OF A JOB INTERVIEW

Q. What does a typical day in this role look like?

Q. What are the key indicators of success in this role?

Q. What are some of the growth opportunities in this role?

Q. What is your favourite part about working at the company?

Q. Can you tell me a bit more about the company culture?

Q. What are the next steps in the process?

Q. What are some things you hope the person in this role will accomplish?

Q. What are some of the company's goals for the next few years?

You've made it. The interview is almost over! Before the interview wraps up, an interviewer will usually ask you if you have any questions for them. Use this opportunity strategically to show that you are genuinely interested in the role and the company, as well as to determine if the job aligns with your goals and values.

Ask two to three questions directly related to the interview, the company, the role and its responsibilities, as well as any points that were not already discussed in the interview. Prepare a few questions before your interview and ask the most relevant ones based on your discussion on the day. Use these examples as a starting point.

WHAT DOES A TYPICAL DAY IN THIS ROLE LOOK LIKE?

By asking this question, you are trying to get more specific context about what your daily activities may involve. While the job description would have given you an understanding of the role and responsibilities, it often does not give enough context about the actual activities you will be doing day to day. Each company may have slightly different expectations, so this question can help you to try and gauge further detail.

WHAT ARE THE KEY INDICATORS OF SUCCESS IN THIS ROLE?

This question aims to understand what the company sees as 'success' in this role. This could include strict key performance indicators (KPIs) or metrics, or it could involve more high-level indicators, such as creativity and innovation. Understanding what the company views as success will ensure that you are both on the same page and can hit the ground running.

WHAT ARE SOME OF THE GROWTH OPPORTUNITIES IN THIS ROLE?

This question emphasises to the interviewer that you want to learn and develop in this role. It also gives them an insight into your attitude and the goals you hope to achieve. As the interviewee, this question will help you ascertain whether the employer encourages growth and development and what opportunities they provide.

WHAT ARE SOME THINGS YOU HOPE THE PERSON IN THIS ROLE WILL ACCOMPLISH?

This question will tell you what the company's plans are for the role currently, and also for the future. There may be some short-term goals that the company has for this role that haven't been discussed or raised so far in the interview process. All jobs are also part of a bigger plan and strategy that a company has in place. By asking this question, you may be able to learn about the longer-term plans for the role and its importance within the broader company.

WHAT ARE SOME OF THE COMPANY'S GOALS FOR THE NEXT FEW YEARS?

This question will help you understand the direction the company is going in to help you figure out if it is a place you will be happy working. It can also help you uncover the direction your specific role will go based on the company's broader goals. Understanding the strategic vision of the company is valuable as it creates a sense of purpose for the role you are applying for.

CAN YOU TELL ME A BIT MORE ABOUT THE COMPANY CULTURE?

A company's culture is everything. A positive culture will make all the difference in being able to enjoy your job. On the other hand, a negative culture will diminish your motivation and enthusiasm for your job. If the interviewer side steps around the question or gives you a generic response, try following up by asking these questions to further prompt them:

- How long have the people in the team been working at the company?
- What is the company's view on work-life balance?
- What does the team do for fun?

These follow-up questions will give you a better idea of whether the company culture is right for you or not.

WHAT IS YOUR FAVOURITE PART ABOUT WORKING AT THE COMPANY?

This question is trying to seek a real-life answer from the interviewer that isn't just what is written in the job advertisement or on the company website. Don't be afraid to continue the conversation from their answer to find out more details about what they find most enjoyable in their role.

WHAT ARE THE NEXT STEPS IN THE PROCESS?

Asking for the next steps in the process shows the interviewer that you are serious and eager for the role. It also gives you an insight into what you can expect moving forward in the process, including the associated timings. All companies do their hiring differently, so knowing the process will help keep you patient and allow you to know when might be the right time to follow up.

AFTER THE INTERVIEW

POST-INTERVIEW THANK YOU

Leave a lasting impression by sending a thank you email to the interviewer within 24 hours of your interview. This email should thank the interviewer for their time, reference discussion points from the interview, emphasise why you are the best candidate for the role and re-confirm your enthusiasm. Use the template below as a starting point.

Subject line: *Your Name: [POSITION TITLE] Position*

Hi [INTERVIEWER NAME],

Thank you for your time [EARLIER/YESTERDAY] to discuss the [POSITION TITLE] position at [COMPANY].

It was great to get an insight into what the role involves and learn more about the team and how the company operates.

The day-to-day responsibilities and the challenges that would be undertaken in this role strongly align with my previous experiences and where I would like to take my career. [INCLUDE EXAMPLES OF ANY CHALLENGES OR RESPONSIBILITIES]

Following our discussion, I am especially excited about the opportunity to work at [COMPANY] and am confident I will be able to work with the team to deliver the desired outcomes in this role. [INCLUDE EXAMPLES OF ANY DESIRED OUTCOMES]

Please don't hesitate to get in touch if you have any more questions.

I look forward to hearing from you.

Kind regards,

[NAME]
[EMAIL] | [PHONE]

FOLLOWING UP

Even though the interview is over, the days after can fill you with anxiety and nerves as you wait to hear back from the company. The recruitment process can take time, especially if it's a larger company. Be flexible with extended timelines, try to be available for any additional interviews and promptly provide any additional information that the company requests from you. Even if this is your dream role, stay active in your job search. Having more job offers on the table gives you greater leverage to negotiate your starting salary.

Generally, the interviewer will tell you when you can expect to hear from them. If you have not heard anything by this time, or you were not given a clear timeline and more than three days have elapsed, send a follow-up email to the hiring manager or recruiter.

Subject line: *Your Name: [POSITION TITLE] Position Follow Up*

Hi [HR MANAGER/INTERVIEWER NAME],

I hope you are having a great week!

I wanted to follow up on the [POSITION TITLE] position and see if there was any update on my application. It was really great to meet with [YOU/ INTERVIEWER NAME] and learn more about the role. I am excited about the opportunity to join [COMPANY] and I appreciate you considering me for this role.

If there is any further information you need or anything more I can do, please let me know.

Kind regards,

[NAME]
[EMAIL] | [PHONE]

ASKING FOR FEEDBACK

Despite your best efforts, sometimes job interviews don't work out. Even if you miss out on the job, you should always ask for feedback from the recruiter or hiring manager to help you improve for future interviews. Ask them what they think you did well, how you can improve for next time, as well as any tips to help you in future interviews.

Subject line: *Your Name: [POSITION TITLE] — Request for Feedback*

Hi [HR MANAGER/INTERVIEWER NAME],

I appreciate your time during the interview process and thank you again for the opportunity to be considered for the role.

While I am disappointed that I was not the best fit for the role, I wish the selected person all the best.

I would really appreciate any feedback on the interview and how I may be able to better position myself for future roles with [COMPANY].

Kind regards,

[NAME]
[EMAIL] | [PHONE]

NEGOTIATING YOUR STARTING SALARY

You made it through the job interview and have received an offer — congratulations! But before you sign on the dotted line, you should always first see if there is any room to negotiate your starting salary and other non-monetary benefits.

I get it—discussing money and your salary can be awkward and uncomfortable.

You might be thinking:

- How much am I worth?
- What if they think I'm being demanding?
- Do they have the budget?
- Will they take my offer away?

To answer your questions:

- A lot, and you deserve to be paid adequately for all the skills and experience you're bringing to the table.
- You're not — negotiation is not meant to be argumentative. It's all about facts and compromise to reach a mutually beneficial outcome.

- You won't know until you ask. Most employers expect you to negotiate, especially after an offer has been made.

- Unlikely. They've picked you and would rather work together to find a suitable salary than restart the recruitment process. If they do revoke your offer, it's not a place you want to work for anyway.

Negotiation feels unnatural to most people, but the good news is that it is a skill that you can develop, improve and master. The more you negotiate, the better you will get at it. Ideally, you want to defer the salary conversation for as long as possible to give yourself time to understand the role and identify the unique strengths, skills and experiences that you will bring to the role. The best time to negotiate your salary is after an offer has been made to you.

If the recruiter or interviewer asks you what salary range you are expecting before you have received an offer, say this:

I'm not clear on the full responsibilities of the role at the moment, but I'm confident that the salary you are offering is competitive in the current market and aligns with my skills and experience.

HOW TO NEGOTIATE YOUR SALARY

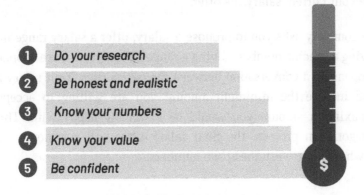

1. Do your research
2. Be honest and realistic
3. Know your numbers
4. Know your value
5. Be confident

1. DO YOUR RESEARCH

Start by researching the current salary trends for the role that you are applying for and understand what other people in the same industry, in the same location and with similar experience and skills are getting paid. Talk to friends in the industry and utilise online tools and websites, such as Glassdoor, Payscale and LinkedIn Salary. Compare the different roles and salaries to gauge an approximate salary range for the role you are applying for. You will be able to use this as a benchmark when negotiating your salary.

2. BE HONEST AND REALISTIC

Based on the research you conducted in step 1, you should now have a solid sense of a *typical* salary range in your field and for your desired position. The next step is to reflect on your own skills and expertise. Evaluate your level of education; additional certifications, training or courses you have completed; responsibilities and accomplishments in other roles; past experiences on similar projects; and any unique knowledge, in-demand skills or abilities that will benefit the company. Review this against the research you did and place yourself in the salary range you established.

3. KNOW YOUR NUMBERS

The next step is actually determining the salary amount that you want to aim for in negotiations. The aim here is to get at least 10 to 20 per cent above your current salary/the offer.

If the company asks you to propose a salary, offer a salary range instead of giving a specific number. Giving a range also appears more cooperative as it opens up a conversation between the two parties. Your salary range should include the minimum amount you are willing to accept and the maximum amount you would be extremely happy with. Through the negotiation process, the final salary offer will commonly end up somewhere in between these two numbers.

4. KNOW YOUR VALUE

At this point, you need to be able to explain to the company that the value you will bring is worth the salary you are trying to negotiate. The most effective way to do this is by showcasing fact-based examples and evidence from your past experiences that are relevant to the role. You have skills and experience, so don't be afraid to show them off! Similar to what you did in your resumé, give examples using real numbers and quantifiable data where you can. Think of times when you have saved your previous employer money or time, increased profits, improved efficiencies or implemented new business strategies.

5. BE CONFIDENT

The final step is staying confident throughout the negotiation process. Negotiating involves a lot of back and forth, so remain patient and calm. Stick to any deadlines and make sure you get everything agreed upon in writing. If the company is unable to offer you a salary increase, you may be able to instead negotiate non-monetary benefits, such as flexible working arrangements, educational opportunities, extra paid leave or a 'better' job title. You can also try proposing a six-month review where the company can assess your performance and a potential pay rise.

Your negotiation journey

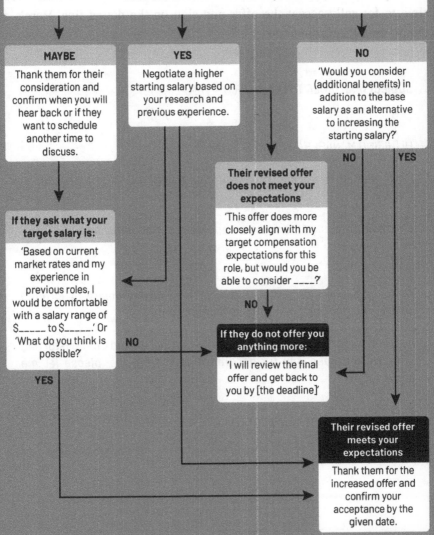

YOU HAVE RECEIVED AN OFFER OVER THE PHONE OR VIA EMAIL

'I am excited about the role and the contribution I can make to [TEAM/COMPANY NAME], however, I want to make sure that I am comfortable with the level of compensation. Would we be able to review the final salary offer?

MAYBE
Thank them for their consideration and confirm when you will hear back or if they want to schedule another time to discuss.

YES
Negotiate a higher starting salary based on your research and previous experience.

NO
'Would you consider (additional benefits) in addition to the base salary as an alternative to increasing the starting salary?

NO   YES

Their revised offer does not meet your expectations

'This offer does more closely align with my target compensation expectations for this role, but would you be able to consider ____?

If they ask what your target salary is:

'Based on current market rates and my experience in previous roles, I would be comfortable with a salary range of $_____ to $_____.' Or 'What do you think is possible?'

NO

If they do not offer you anything more:

'I will review the final offer and get back to you by [the deadline]'

YES

NO

Their revised offer meets your expectations

Thank them for the increased offer and confirm your acceptance by the given date.

RESPONDING TO A JOB OFFER

ACCEPTING A JOB OFFER

When you are happy with the final offer and terms of your contract, it's time to formally accept the offer and sign on the dotted line. Here's a simple email template to use.

> **Subject line:** [ROLE TITLE] Position — [YOUR NAME]
>
> ---
>
> Hi [HIRING MANAGER/RECRUITER NAME],
>
> I am excited to accept your offer for the [ROLE TITLE] position at [COMPANY].
>
> Please find attached the accepted and signed offer agreement.
>
> [OR]
>
> As we previously discussed, I accept the starting salary of [offered salary] and [include any additional benefits agreed].
>
> I look forward to meeting the team and getting started on the [starting date]. If you need any further information from me, please let me know.
>
> Kind regards,
>
> [YOUR NAME]

DECLINING A JOB OFFER

Sometimes a company cannot meet your minimum requirements or you may have received an offer from another company that you would prefer to take. If this is the case, it's important to let the company know as soon as possible that you will be declining their job offer. Be polite and courteous in this email and offer to stay connected via LinkedIn. You may choose to provide a reason for declining the offer (e.g. that you accepted a position elsewhere), but this is entirely optional.

You can use the template below to politely decline a job offer.

Subject line: *[ROLE TITLE] Position — [YOUR NAME]*

Hi [HIRING MANAGER/RECRUITER NAME],

Thank you for offering me the [ROLE TITLE] position. It has been great to learn more about [COMPANY] and the work that you do.

Unfortunately, I am unable to accept the position at this time.

I appreciate your consideration of me for this position and thank you for the opportunity and for your time during this interview process. All the best with the work you are doing at [COMPANY] and I look forward to staying connected.

Kind regards,

[YOUR NAME]

RESIGNING ON GOOD TERMS

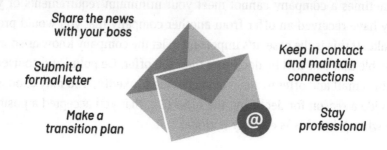

Share the news with your boss

Submit a formal letter

Make a transition plan

Keep in contact and maintain connections

@

Stay professional

Whether you love or hate your existing role or manager, resigning from your job can feel daunting. I know it is easier said than done, but try not to let your emotions get the better of you. Resigning on good terms will give you confidence during the transition that you have made the right decision and are closing the chapter on that role.

SHARE THE NEWS WITH YOUR BOSS

Avoid catching your manager or boss off guard and, instead, schedule a quick catch-up meeting with them. It can be difficult to know how your boss will take the news. Prepare to be hit with: 'What can we do to make you stay?' (a bit late now…), or worse, 'You're making the wrong decision'. Stay calm, polite and keep it as brief as possible. It may seem like a good opportunity to air everything that's wrong with the company and the annoying people you have had to work with, but it's best to keep the conversation about you and your career pathway.

SUBMIT A FORMAL LETTER

It is always a good idea to submit a formal resignation letter so the company has a record of your resignation. You can either bring this with you to the meeting with your boss or email it afterwards. Your resignation letter should be short and include key details such as your last official day of work. Take a look at your employment agreement to check that you are in line with your resignation notice terms (and while you're there, check your accrued leave payment rights and any other conditions you may benefit from).

Here is a resignation letter template you can use.

Subject line: *Resignation Letter: [YOUR NAME]*

Hi [BOSS' NAME],

Please accept this letter as formal notice of my resignation from my position as [POSITION TITLE] at [COMPANY]. My last day of employment will be [DATE].

Thank you for the opportunity to work at [COMPANY] over the past [NUMBER OF YEARS/MONTHS]. I have enjoyed working here and appreciate all the support and guidance the team has given me during this time; however, I have decided it is time for me to move on to my next challenge.

Thank you again for the opportunity and I wish you and the team all the best for the future.

Yours sincerely,

[YOUR NAME]

MAKE A TRANSITION PLAN

It is important to consider how you will hand over your work to your team or the next person taking over your job. A transition plan is a document that summarises what you do every day in your role, including all those random tasks that just appeared over time that don't seem to be in your job description. It should include your standard duties and responsibilities, the additional tasks you do outside of your role, all the current projects or activities you are currently working on and any key contacts or tips you have for the role. It is also beneficial to make a list of the outstanding tasks you are planning to complete before you leave and provide a status of the list to your team or manager in the last few days before you go. Start this process as soon as possible so you can enjoy your final day without any stress.

STAY PROFESSIONAL

As tempting as it may be, don't start badmouthing your existing employer. Always maintain a positive and professional attitude. Any final words you have for your employer will leave a lasting impression that can either work for or against you in the future.

If you have feedback that you would like to give or you need to raise serious concerns, schedule a meeting with HR or the relevant manager to discuss it. Workplaces will often conduct an exit interview or ask that you complete an exit survey where you can share your experiences.

KEEP IN CONTACT AND MAINTAIN CONNECTIONS

You never know when you will cross paths with or need to reconnect with colleagues and mentors again. People move around in their careers so staying connected may lead to your next big role or help you find employees when you become a manager yourself. Ask for people's personal email addresses and connect with them on LinkedIn.

7

Confidence at work

POWERFUL WORK AFFIRMATIONS

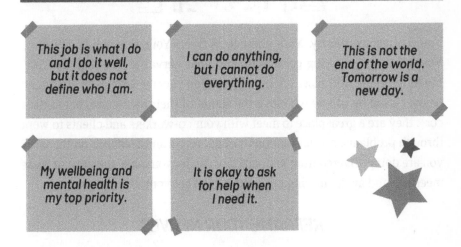

This job is what I do and I do it well, but it does not define who I am.

I can do anything, but I cannot do everything.

This is not the end of the world. Tomorrow is a new day.

My wellbeing and mental health is my top priority.

It is okay to ask for help when I need it.

If there is only one thing you learn from this book, let it be this: *Stop attaching your identity, your worth or your happiness to your job.*

Your job is simply one aspect of your life. It's where you work hard in exchange for monetary and non-monetary benefits. So why is it that so many of us associate our personal success directly with our career? I'm not saying you shouldn't try your best at work, but your best does not mean compromising your happiness or health. Instead, prioritise what matters most—looking after yourself, fulfilling your purpose, spending time with loved ones and making lifelong memories.

Whenever work is challenging you, read the above affirmations. You may only resonate with one or two, but take a deep breath and say them out loud. Repeat as often as necessary.

OVERCOMING MEETING ANXIETY

Your palms are sweaty. Your chest feels tight. Your stomach is churning. You have a big meeting coming up and your nerves are through the roof. Meetings in the workplace are inevitable. Don't get me wrong, meetings can be over-used by people who love the sound of their own voice, but at their core, they are a great place to meet with your co-workers and clients to work through problems, create solutions and get important feedback on the work you are doing. Overcoming your anxiety can let you make the most of these meetings and avoid missing opportunities to get your ideas across.

REFRAME YOUR NERVES

Prior to the meeting, think about what exactly is making you nervous about the meeting. Are you not confident with the topic? Is it with a new client you are trying to impress? Are you concerned about the outcome? Most of the time, we are nervous because we want the meeting to go well. Reframe your nerves as showing how much you care for the work you do.

GROUND YOURSELF

Find a strategy that works for you to ground yourself and calm your nerves. As a first step, try doing some focused breathing exercises, doing 5 star jumps or repeating a positive affirmation.

PREPARE AND PRACTISE BEFOREHAND

Gather your notes, go over the meeting agenda and make sure your tech is working correctly. Practise your presentation out loud before the meeting and prepare the questions you would like to ask and have covered.

SPEAK UP EARLY AND TAKE NOTES

Speak up early in the meeting to take the pressure off. Speaking up early can also set the tone of the meeting and direct the conversation to where you would like it to go. If you don't get the chance to share your ideas during the meeting, send an email afterwards with your thoughts.

BE CONFIDENT IN YOUR CONTRIBUTIONS

Remind yourself that your contributions are valid and insightful. You are in the meeting for a reason, and your ideas and thoughts could be the important information that is required for the discussion.

STAY ENGAGED AND FOLLOW UP

Listen closely to the other meeting attendees and stay engaged with the conversation. Actively listening to the conversation will help with how and when you would like to contribute your ideas. Take notes during the meeting and email these notes, any relevant additional information (like the meeting slides) and a list of action items around to the attendees after wards. This will give you confidence that the meeting was productive and you covered everything that was required.

How to sound more confident at work

❌	✔️
This is probably a silly question but...	I'm still wrapping my head around this; can you please explain x further?
No worries/no problem!	Always happy to help!
I just wanted to check in	I wanted to check in (remove just)
Is this what you wanted?	Let me know if this is what you had in mind
Does that make sense?	What are your thoughts?
I'm not sure if this is right, but...	Based on my past experience, the best approach is...
Sorry, I didn't realise	Thanks for pointing that out
I feel that maybe we should...	I recommend that we...
What works best for you?	Can you do [time]?

How to sound more confident at work

❌	✔️
I don't understand	Can you please clarify what you mean?
Sorry to bother you	Can you please help with this?
I'm not sure if that is correct	Before we move on, I want to confirm...
I'm not sure	Let me get back to you and confirm that by [time]
I think we should also do...	I have two areas of improvement to add to that
Is it okay if I leave early?	I will need to leave at [time] for...
Hopefully that makes sense?	Let me know if you have any questions
Sorry for the delay	Thank you for your patience
I think we could improve this by...	What I would like to see here is...

WHEN TO SAY 'NO' AT WORK

- The task interferes with your actual responsibilities
- The deadline is unrealistic
- You're on leave
- You're being taken advantage of
- You're not qualified (or the best qualified) to complete the task
- You're asked to do something unethical/unsafe

Saying 'no' at work is hard, especially when you are early in your career or you are really passionate about what you do. Often there is a huge amount of guilt attached, questioning whether you are a team player or not wanting to let your manager down.

But learning when to say 'no' is one of the most important skills to learn in the workplace. Not only does it protect you from being overworked and taken advantage of, but it also helps protect the passion and drive you have for your job. Too often, eager employees are cursed with saying 'yes' to everything, leading them to be exhausted, frustrated and resenting the job that they once loved.

Other times, you may find yourself subject to poor management or unethical behaviour if you are asked to complete a task that you know you shouldn't be doing. Saying 'no' sets a strong boundary with the asker and reinforces that their request is wrong.

HOW TO SAY 'NO' AT WORK

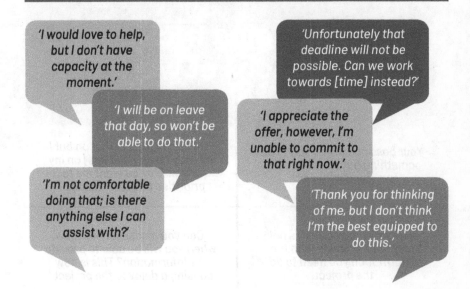

'I would love to help, but I don't have capacity at the moment.'

'Unfortunately that deadline will not be possible. Can we work towards [time] instead?'

'I will be on leave that day, so won't be able to do that.'

'I appreciate the offer, however, I'm unable to commit to that right now.'

'I'm not comfortable doing that; is there anything else I can assist with?'

'Thank you for thinking of me, but I don't think I'm the best equipped to do this.'

Now that you know *when* to say no at work, *how* do you actually do it? Getting comfortable with saying 'no' to your boss, colleague or client takes practice. Be polite and don't over-explain yourself. You are setting a boundary to protect your time and energy, so be confident and stay firm if there is any push back. Having a strong understanding of why you are saying no to the request will allow you to do so without feeling guilty.

Managing tricky situations at work

SITUATION	WHAT TO SAY
Your boss has asked you to do something but you're already swamped with work.	'I'm happy to take that on but I already have [list tasks] on my plate. Did you want me to prioritise this task instead?'
Your colleague/client is not responding to you with the information you need to do the project.	'Can you please let me know when you will be able to provide the information? This is now causing a delay to the project.'
You've been asked to help with something that is not your job.	'This is not something I typically do, but I am happy to connect you with someone who can help.'
Another unnecessary meeting has been scheduled.	'Before jumping into a meeting to discuss this, can we please confirm the intent and outcome we are aiming for?'
Your boss has asked you to stay back to finish something that is not urgent.	'I will get this done first thing tomorrow morning.'
Your client is not responding to your email.	'Can we please set up a quick meeting to discuss this and confirm an outcome moving forward?'

Managing tricky situations at work

SITUATION	WHAT TO SAY
Your colleague is asking you to do their job for them.	'I am at capacity with my own work at the moment, but I can support you where possible.'
Your client/team member keeps bothering you for updates.	'I am still working through this and will provide an update once one is available.'
Your boss keeps trying to micromanage you.	'I am confident in delivering this work and will let you know if I have any questions or need support.'
Your boss/client hasn't given you enough detail to do the task.	'Can you please clarify the details for this task so I can be sure to cover everything that is required.'
Someone has taken credit for your idea.	'Thank you for sharing my idea with the group. It would be great if you could please include me in the delivery in future or discuss this directly with me prior.'
Someone who is not your boss or in your team assigns you a task.	'Can we please discuss this with [manager's name] as I have some ongoing priorities that clash with the work you would like me to do.'

Managing tricky situations at work

SITUATION	WHAT TO SAY
Your colleague is not doing their part fast enough so you can progress with your part.	'Are you still on track to meet the [insert deadline]? I will still need [insert time] to complete my part.'
Your client/colleague has asked you for information you have already provided.	'We provided that information earlier in the attached email, but please see below for convenience.'
Your colleague is not doing their job.	'How are you going with [task]? Let me know if you need some help or if we need to chat with [manager's name] to get some support.'
Your colleague has come to you with an issue that is not your problem.	'I recommend directing this to [name] as they will be better placed to help you.'
Your colleague keeps interrupting you.	'Before you jump in, [insert name], I wanted to finish my point.'

BOUNCING BACK AFTER MAKING A MISTAKE AT WORK

1. *Accept the mistake — Don't feel bad about yourself. Mistakes happen.*

2. *Own up to your mistake: Be honest and tell your manager/boss.*

3. *Focus on the solution: How can you fix the mistake or mitigate the damage caused?*

4. *Learn from the experience: What can you do differently next time so it doesn't happen again?*

Making a mistake at work can take a toll on your self-confidence and leave you questioning your ability in your job. Recovering from a mistake can take time, but being able to bounce back will boost your confidence and allow you to grow both personally and professionally. You will make plenty of mistakes during your career, no matter what rank or stage you are at, so it's important to familiarise yourself with the mistake cycle and embrace the situation as a learning opportunity instead of a setback.

ACCEPT THE MISTAKE

First things first: accept that you made a mistake. Every single person in this world makes mistakes so there is no point trying to hide it, blame someone else or feel sorry for yourself.

OWN UP TO YOUR MISTAKE

Once you have accepted that you have made a mistake, take ownership of it. Be completely honest about the situation with your boss and explain what went wrong. It's always good to come to these discussions with some ideas on how to fix the problem, instead of simply waiting for them to tell you what to do.

FOCUS ON THE SOLUTION

In reality, 99 per cent of problems can be solved. It may feel like the end of the world in the moment, but focus on how you can remedy the situation as quickly as possible. Who do you need to talk to? What actions need to take place? Do you need to raise the issue with a client, manager or other employees?

You may have fixed the mistake immediately after it happened, but there might be further actions that need to take place to contain the after effects and avoid further damage. It is always best to report a mistake even if it has already been fixed.

LEARN FROM THE EXPERIENCE

A mistake usually means something could have been done differently. After the mistake is remedied, think about what you can take away from the experience. Can the process be improved so this doesn't happen again in the future? Is there any way that this mistake could have been caught before it happened? Was the right person doing the right job? Was this human error caused by fatigue? Taking a step back and viewing the mistake from a process improvement perspective can help spotlight company weaknesses and unresolved issues.

From a personal perspective, it is also beneficial to get a different outlook on the experience by talking to other employees, a mentor or a partner who may have made similar mistakes in the past and can provide their learnings from the event.

STOP OVER-APOLOGISING AT WORK

SORRY
SORRY
SORRY

'Thank you for noticing the error. I will ...'

'I am still working through this and will aim to get it to you by [time].'

'Good pick up. I will make the changes now.'

'Thank you for helping me understand how I can improve for next time ...'

'Thank you for waiting. I appreciate your patience.'

'Do you have a minute for a quick question?'

Put your hand up if you're a serial over-apologiser. Don't get me wrong — sometimes an apology is definitely warranted, especially if you make a significant mistake or have done something wrong. But most of the time, we apologise for things we don't need to, which ends up making us feel less confident and questioning ourselves and our abilities.

Next time you need some help or you're working through a task or you make a minor error in a report, instead of saying 'sorry', try these phrases instead.

DEALING WITH IMPOSTER SYNDROME

- *If you weren't ready, you wouldn't have the opportunity.*

- *It's not luck. You have worked hard for this.*

- *You are worthy of good things.*

- *Your voice and perspective is unique.*

- *You will never feel fully 'ready'. Just take the first step.*

Imposter syndrome needs no introduction. If you Google the term, you'll find millions of articles and stories on even the most famous celebrities and public figures experiencing it. We are our own biggest enemy and the voice inside our heads telling us that we 'aren't good enough' or 'not worthy' can seriously hold us back from reaching our full potential.

The next time you are filled with self-doubt or start convincing yourself that you are a fraud, read the reminders above. Challenge the validity of the thoughts in your head. Let go of the constant comparison and need for perfectionism. Write a list of all your accomplishments in the last 12 months, and take a step back to celebrate and be proud of your successes. You are worthy. You are unique. And you are deserving of every good thing that comes your way.

ADVOCATING FOR YOURSELF AT WORK

Put yourself forward for new challenges and opportunities

Remind yourself of everything you have achieved

Have open discussions with your manager about your performance

Don't be scared to ask for what you want and negotiate where possible

Share your knowledge and experiences with your team

Form genuine relationships with your co-workers

Advocating for yourself at work is all about taking your career into your own hands. Your hard work and accomplishments should be progressing you towards your career goals and make you feel confident and fulfilled in the workplace.

PUT YOURSELF FORWARD FOR NEW CHALLENGES AND OPPORTUNITIES

You are your own best advocate at work, so make it known to your manager and team that you are open to new challenges and opportunities. If possible, be specific about the new opportunities that you want to explore, such as trying a project with a different team or taking on a new client in an industry you haven't worked in before. If your manager is aware of your career goals and your eagerness to try new things, you are more likely to be given new opportunities.

HAVE OPEN DISCUSSIONS WITH YOUR MANAGER
ABOUT YOUR PERFORMANCE

If you don't have frequent performance review discussions with your manager already set in your calendar, get on your computer and schedule a check-in right now. Your manager needs to know what your career goals are and how they can best assist you with reaching those goals. These discussions are also important to track your performance and openly discuss pathways for promotions and career development. Set a meeting, set some goals and create a plan with your manager to outline how you will achieve them.

SHARE YOUR KNOWLEDGE AND EXPERIENCES
WITH YOUR TEAM

Whenever you learn something new or discover a fresh way to do something, share it with your team. Maybe you discovered a new Excel shortcut that halved the amount of time to do something, or maybe you started sharing a weekly report with a client that is working really well. Whatever it is, sharing your knowledge and experiences helps to strengthen team morale and improve the skills of the whole team.

Don't forget to also share any specific knowledge and experience you have on certain subjects. This will position you as a subject matter expert, and you will be called upon for opportunities that require your expertise.

REMIND YOURSELF OF EVERYTHING
YOU HAVE ACHIEVED

Take some time once a week to check in with yourself and reflect on everything you have achieved. Track your performance against your goals, and keep yourself accountable for when it is time to have discussions with your manager about your role. Understanding how you are performing will give you the confidence to advocate for yourself in the workplace.

DON'T BE SCARED TO ASK FOR WHAT YOU WANT AND NEGOTIATE WHERE POSSIBLE

The reality in most workplaces is that if you don't ask, you won't receive. Be vocal and put your hand up for new opportunities, highlight your desire to go for promotion, and negotiate pay rises based on your performance and achievements. Be transparent with your manager and have regular, open conversations with them about your career goals and objectives.

FORM GENUINE RELATIONSHIPS WITH YOUR CO-WORKERS

We often spend more time with our co-workers than we do with our own friends and family, so it's important to build positive and genuine relationships with them. There are many benefits of strong working relationships, including:

- creating a support system for yourself
- increased sense of belonging
- reduced workplace stress
- greater job satisfaction and engagement
- decreased job turnover
- better collaboration and team outcomes
- increased productivity and motivation.

Not only does getting along with your team make work more enjoyable, but the lifelong connections can help you in your career down the track.

ACCEPTING A COMPLIMENT AT WORK

'Thank you. The whole team worked really hard to get the job done.'

'Thank you. I really appreciate you taking the time to let me know.'

'You're welcome. I'm glad I could help out.'

'I put a lot of effort into the presentation. Thank you for noticing.'

'Thank you. I'm happy with how the work turned out.'

Or just a simple 'Thank you!'

When someone at work compliments you, your natural instinct may be to brush it off or downplay your achievement. Instead, accept the compliment graciously and be appreciative of their kind words. Smile and say 'thank you' — you deserve it!

And don't forget, whenever you receive a compliment or positive feedback, save the email in a folder and log it in your accomplishments tracker to use as evidence for when you go for a promotion or pay rise (more on this in chapter 8).

TACKLING SCARY CONVERSATIONS AT WORK

1. *Prepare and practise beforehand*

2. *Know what outcome/solution you want*

3. *Find the right time*

4. *Be open to discussion*

5. *Finish with a solution*

6. *Follow up and check-in*

There will be many times throughout your career when you will need to have a scary conversation. Whether you are asking for a pay rise, raising a complaint or advocating for a change, these conversations all require planning, execution and accountability. Be confident when tackling scary conversations at work by following these steps.

PREPARE AND PRACTISE BEFOREHAND

Prepare for the conversation by listing out your points and practising what you want to say. This will help you focus on the facts and not get caught up in the emotions of the situation.

KNOW WHAT OUTCOME/SOLUTION YOU WANT

Before going into the conversation, you need to decide on the exact outcome you want. Are you looking for a specific decision then and there? Do you want to create an action plan to resolve the situation you are discussing? Does the person need to come back to you with some more information? Knowing the outcome you want will give the person clear actions to follow after the discussion.

FIND THE RIGHT TIME

Find time in the person's calendar and set up a meeting. Include a subject line or detail in the invitation to give them some context (e.g. [Your Name] Performance Discussion or Team Resources Discussion). You want the person to be prepared and focused for what you want to discuss — catching your boss two minutes before a meeting is not ideal.

BE OPEN TO DISCUSSION

During the conversation, be sure to listen and let the person respond to the points you have made. You are trying to get an outcome or resolution from them, so they need to be part of the dialogue.

FINISH WITH A SOLUTION

Before letting the conversation finish up, make sure to set out and agree on the steps forward. If you aren't getting a clear response from the person, ask them specifically, 'Can you please let me know the next steps so we can resolve this together?'

FOLLOW UP AND CHECK-IN

Don't go silent after a serious conversation. Follow up with the person, either formally or informally, and re-visit the outcome and plan that you established at the end of the first conversation. This is the point of reference to keep that person accountable for the actions that they agreed to.

8

Your career pathway

FIGURING OUT YOUR CAREER PATHWAY

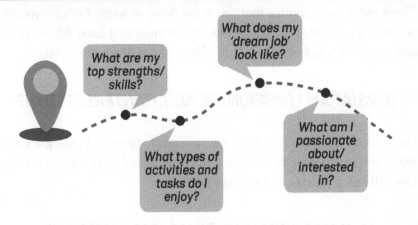

What are my top strengths/skills?

What types of activities and tasks do I enjoy?

What does my 'dream job' look like?

What am I passionate about/ interested in?

How does life go from answering 'What do you want to be when you grow up?' to 'What am I even doing with my career?'. Many of us probably assumed that we would graduate high school, study something we are passionate about at university and then pursue a long, fulfilling career in that field.

But life is way more complicated and nuanced than that. Firstly, many roles are completely different in practice from what we see in TV shows or imagine in our heads. And, secondly, the world of work is rapidly changing and half the roles available today did not even exist five years ago. This makes it hard to know exactly how to navigate our career and find a pathway that is both impactful and fulfilling. If you have no idea what you are doing with your career, the best place to start is by asking yourself the following four questions.

1. WHAT ARE MY TOP STRENGTHS/SKILLS?

Make a list of both your top hard skills (i.e. technical skills) and soft skills (i.e. people skills). If you get stuck, think about what your colleagues or people in your life ask for your help with or tell you that you are really good at.

2. WHAT TYPES OF ACTIVITIES AND TASKS DO I ENJOY?

Think about the activities that you enjoy doing at work. Perhaps you like presenting to clients? Or writing reports? Or analysing data? Also consider any activities or hobbies you enjoy doing outside of work as well.

3. WHAT AM I PASSIONATE ABOUT/INTERESTED IN?

Do you love fitness? Or maybe you're a music fanatic? Finding a career that incorporates your passions and interests increases the likelihood that you will enjoy the role and stay motivated.

4. WHAT DOES MY 'DREAM JOB' LOOK LIKE?

This question is all about your career values. Take a moment and visualise your 'dream job'. What is the work environment like? What is the dress code? How big is the team? Is the role flexible? How much responsibility do you have? Be as specific as possible when describing your dream role. These values will underpin your entire career pathway.

Next, brainstorm some possible industries/companies/career options that combine your answers to the above questions. For example, let's say you are highly skilled and enjoy doing data analysis, but you are also passionate about the beauty industry. Can you find a data analyst role at a beauty company?

It's also important to remind yourself that finding your career pathway will involve trial and error. There will be many occasions where a role looks great on paper but won't meet your expectations in reality. Be patient with yourself, keep trying new things and don't put a timeline on finding your dream job.

SIGNS YOU MAY BE STUCK IN YOUR CURRENT JOB

Completely unmotivated

Not aligned with your values

Company can't provide a clear career path for you

Don't see a future there

Dread going into work every day

There is no change in pay, title or tasks

Not feeling challenged

Ideas to help are being ignored

Can't be authentic at work

Health is declining

Manager does not respect your role

Work culture is toxic

No desire to grow or learn more

Over-complain to your partner

Constantly browsing job sites

No recognition for hard work

Feel like your talents are being wasted

Lack of support from management

STOP

Are you feeling stuck in your job at the moment? I'm sure it took you less than a second to answer that question. It's completely normal to feel stuck in a role, even if you once really loved it or you expected it to be your dream job. The good news is that you don't have to stay stuck forever, and there's a range of options available to you if you need to shake things up. Firstly, take a moment to reflect on these warning signs that you may be stuck in your job. If one resonates with you, write down specific examples of this happening in your current work situation.

WHAT TO DO IF YOU FEEL STUCK IN YOUR JOB

1. Find the root of the problem

2. Evaluate your options internally

3. Talk to a variety of people

4. Learn a new skill

5. Start a side hustle

6. Explore new job opportunities

Once you recognise why you are feeling stuck in your job, it's time to take action and make a change. There's no black-and-white answer to becoming 'un-stuck'. Instead, here are six options to explore and see what works best for your personal situation.

1. FIND THE ROOT OF THE PROBLEM

Start off by diving deep into the exact reasons why you feel stuck in your job. Look back at the signs on page 131 and write a list of everything you do and don't like about your job. Be as detailed as possible — were there specific situations that bothered you? Is it the work or the people in your team that are the underlying issue? Are there certain things keeping you there?

2. EVALUATE YOUR OPTIONS INTERNALLY

Can you try a new project that involves working with colleagues from other teams? Does your company have different departments that you could move to internally? If you aren't clear on what the other areas of the company do, speak with your manager to see if there's any possibility of setting up some internal work experience to gain an insight into what the other teams do on an everyday basis. You can also explore whether your employer offers any training or external learning opportunities that could assist you with changing roles within the company.

3. TALK TO A VARIETY OF PEOPLE

Talk to people in your network and ask what they do for work and what they love about what they do. Connect with new people through professional social networks and by attending networking events/seminars. Ask them about their job and what advice they can provide about working in their role/industry.

4. LEARN A NEW SKILL

Look for in-person workshops or online platforms to learn new skills in an area you find interesting. There are plenty of free options out there like YouTube or free Skillshare trials, so start there if you don't have any clear ideas. Don't be afraid to keep trying new things — you may find a hidden talent or passion you didn't realise you had.

5. START A SIDE HUSTLE

Starting a side hustle is another way that you can explore your passion and potentially turn it into your full-time job. Growing a side hustle outside of your work hours is a great way to test out a new career path while still receiving a steady pay cheque from your regular job.

If all else fails, it's time to start applying for new jobs. Go back to chapter 6 to help you navigate your next career move.

HOW TO CHANGE CAREER PATHS

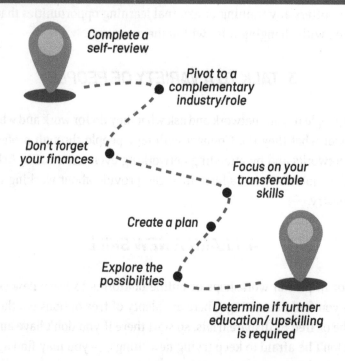

Complete a self-review

Pivot to a complementary industry/role

Don't forget your finances

Focus on your transferable skills

Create a plan

Explore the possibilities

Determine if further education/ upskilling is required

Whether you are stuck in a job that you have lost passion for or you are just ready for a fresh start and a new challenge, changing career paths should be a thoughtful and considered process. It starts with understanding your personal needs, then researching your options and, finally, creating an action plan for how to make it happen.

COMPLETE A SELF-REVIEW

First, you must take stock of your career journey to date and assess your experiences. Understand what makes you happy in the workplace, and what work activities you do and don't like. Review your skill set, interests and values, and how they may fit into a new career role. Refer back to the 'Figuring out your career pathway' activity on page 129 for more.

PIVOT TO A COMPLEMENTARY INDUSTRY/ROLE

Changing career paths does not always mean moving to a completely new industry. It is worthwhile considering whether there are any overlapping industries to the one you are in now to make your transition easier. For example, you may be a consultant who works with a variety of healthcare clients. Moving to a new position within the healthcare industry is a much easier move to make given your previous experience. Alternatively, you can also look at common roles within different industries to allow yourself to best leverage your existing skills and experience to secure your next role. For example, if you're currently working as a project manager in the construction industry, looking for similar roles in a new industry means the transition will be more seamless.

FOCUS ON YOUR TRANSFERABLE SKILLS

Transferable skills are gained through various activities both inside and outside of your formal employment. These skills may have been developed in one environment but can be transferred to benefit another (e.g. your next role!). Some examples of transferable skills include customer service, teamwork, problem-solving, planning, communication, budgeting, flexibility in starting and completing a project, and presenting. Even if you haven't had any direct experience when changing career paths and applying for a new role, you can focus on the transferable skills that you possess to make the hiring manager confident that you have what it takes to be successful in the role. Write out a list of the transferable skills you possess and refer back to these as you look for jobs in a new industry or field.

EXPLORE THE POSSIBILITIES

Whether you decide to change industries completely or stick with something you are familiar with, you need to understand what potential jobs exist in the market and the different career pathways available with these roles. Do a search of all the open job opportunities in the industry or at the specific company you are wanting to move into to get an idea of what sort of roles are available.

To get a real-life understanding of career pathways, look at the LinkedIn profile of someone who works in the position you would like to move into, and review the career pathway that led them to that role. For more specific details, get in touch with the company's HR team and ask how the role you are interested in fits into their company's organisational structure and how their career progression is managed.

DETERMINE IF FURTHER EDUCATION OR UPSKILLING IS REQUIRED

Read through the position descriptions of the jobs you want to apply for and match these against your existing qualifications, experiences and skill set. Are there any gaps in your current experience or skill set that may hold you back? Do you need any further formal qualifications to qualify for these positions? List all of the further education and upskilling that you require to give yourself the best opportunity to successfully make a transition.

CREATE A PLAN

It's time to bring your career change research together and create an action plan. Once you have a specific role or industry in mind, the next step is to map out how you will make the transition happen. Write a list of all the tasks required to make this career change, including any upskilling and further education activities, updating your resumé, attending industry events, networking, meeting informally with hiring managers and recruiters, preparing job applications and landing your career-changing role. Map these activities out into a timeline and set clear milestones to achieve them.

DON'T FORGET YOUR FINANCES

Lastly, consider whether this career change will impact your finances. Are you looking at a big pay increase or a pay cut? If you are anticipating a big pay cut, build up an emergency fund with three to six months of your essential living expenses so you can feel confident that your career change won't impact your day-to-day livelihood. Don't forget to also review your budget and re-establish how you will manage your expenses on your new salary.

If you are expecting a pay increase with this career change, review your budget and re-allocate your income so you aren't going to be impacted by lifestyle creep. While you deserve to treat yourself for making the big move, don't let the pay increase get you into a worse financial position.

COMMUNITY STORY
Switching paths

I was in a career that didn't satisfy me for six years. The kind of situation where you cry before work but you keep going because it pays well.

I saw the SWS community on Instagram and I bought the Ultimate Money Makeover Game Plan and Wealth Building Dashboard. For the first time in my life I was able to take control of my budget.

I felt powerful and like I was controlling my future.

(continued)

By learning to control my finances, I was inspired to see if I could alter my budget to facilitate a career change. I'm happy to say that I am in my second week of an entry-level IT job, and I've enrolled in further university studies. Best decision I ever made! All of which, I feel, would have been unlikely had I not stumbled upon the SWS page.

Thank you so much for the work you do!

Brenda

IMPORTANT SKILLS FOR CAREER SUCCESS

- ✅ *Always be curious and willing to learn new things*
- ✅ *Set work boundaries and prioritise rest*
- ✅ *Don't be afraid to ask questions*
- ✅ *Learn how to manage your time and prioritise tasks*
- ✅ *Find mentors and build a strong network*

You will need many skills if you want to be successful in your career. These skills are broken down within the various chapters of this book, so you can always refer back to them whenever you need motivation or practical tips and guidance. But to summarise: stay curious. Have a growth mindset. Never stop learning. Prioritise your mental and physical health. Learn how to say no. Remind yourself that it is okay not to know everything. Listen to understand and not just to respond. Step outside of your comfort zone. Document all your work wins. Find your support team. Take risks, but also learn how to have fun.

NETWORKING TIPS

- *Push yourself out of your comfort zone*
- *Be open and genuine*
- *Utilise LinkedIn*
- *Make it a two-way street*
- *Focus on quality, not quantity*
- *Network vertically and horizontally*
- *Follow up*

You may have heard the saying that 'your network is your net worth'. Networking is an essential skill that you need to develop no matter what field or industry you are in. There are numerous benefits of networking, including:

- meeting interesting people with fresh ideas and perspectives
- increasing your visibility and building your brand
- boosting your confidence and communication skills
- receiving career advice and support
- opening doors to new opportunities
- building long-lasting relationships
- advancing your career.

PUSH YOURSELF OUT OF YOUR COMFORT ZONE

No matter how old or experienced you are, networking is scary. But it's important to push yourself out of your comfort zone and remember that the benefits of networking far outweigh the negatives. Attend a variety of networking events and see what types of events you feel most comfortable at. Perhaps you enjoy lunch-and-learn events or speed networking or joining an online community. Whatever it is, challenge yourself on each occasion to speak with one new person and nurture that connection (read on for more tips on how to do this).

BE OPEN AND GENUINE

Skip the rehearsed elevator pitches and instead focus on being yourself when networking. Ask lots of questions and practise active listening to get to know the person and their career history. People connect with people, so be genuine and curious to learn about the other person.

UTILISE LINKEDIN

Being active on LinkedIn is a must when networking. Connect with new people, read up on industry news and trends and share your own updates about your career journey. Many roles are also filled through LinkedIn, so it pays to post regularly and nurture your network.

MAKE IT A TWO-WAY STREET

Don't go into networking expecting to get something out of it. Your focus should be on expanding your horizons and getting to know new people, and positive outcomes will naturally flow from that. Avoid asking for job opportunities or favours without offering any value in return. Networking should be mutually beneficial, not a one-way transaction.

FOCUS ON QUALITY, NOT QUANTITY

Instead of always looking for new connections and networking events, focus on cultivating and strengthening your existing relationships. If someone you met recommended a certain book, reach out to let them know your thoughts after reading it. If you notice that there is an opportunity that one of your contacts would be perfect for, recommend them for it. One strong connection is worth more than 10 acquaintances.

NETWORK VERTICALLY AND HORIZONTALLY

Network with people in all directions. Create connections with those more senior, junior and on the same level as you. Network with people within your team as well as in other teams and industries. Stay open minded when building your network as you never know when the connection may come in handy in the future.

FOLLOW UP

The biggest rule of successful networking — always follow up. If you meet someone in person, ask to connect with them on LinkedIn or send them an email expressing how it was lovely to have met and spoken with them. Stay in touch by interacting with their LinkedIn posts and sharing things that you think might help or interest them.

TRACKING YOUR ACCOMPLISHMENTS

Learning how to track, communicate and celebrate your accomplishments at work is one of the most important career skills you need to develop. There are several reasons why you should routinely track your accomplishments, such as to:

- have a record of all your achievements
- optimise the success of your performance reviews
- use it as evidence when going for a promotion or pay rise
- boost your confidence and motivation
- help you easily update your resumé
- assist you when applying for awards/scholarships/programs.

HOW TO TRACK YOUR ACCOMPLISHMENTS

First, determine how you will track your accomplishments. There's no right or wrong way to do it — pick whatever method works best for you. Here are some ideas:

- Word document

- Excel spreadsheet

- Notes app on your phone

- handwritten in a notebook or journal

- special email folder.

Secondly, split your document/spreadsheet/page into three columns:

1. accomplishments and results you have achieved at work

2. feedback from key stakeholders you worked with on projects

3. any additional tasks and activities you completed where you went above and beyond.

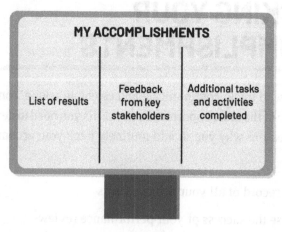

MY ACCOMPLISHMENTS

List of results	Feedback from key stakeholders	Additional tasks and activities completed

Thirdly, spend a few minutes each week updating these columns with examples. Use numbers and quantify your results as much as possible. Save any emails or files that back up these accomplishments in a special folder to refer to when necessary.

PREPARING FOR A PERFORMANCE REVIEW

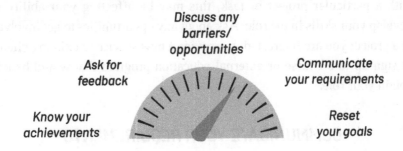

Discuss any
barriers/
opportunities

Ask for
feedback

Communicate
your requirements

Know your
achievements

Reset
your goals

Performance reviews are one of the most important communication tools that both you and your boss can utilise. It is important to understand that these reviews are not just about your performance; they're also a chance for you to set goals with your boss and keep them accountable for their side of the relationship. While most companies implement an annual, biannual or quarterly review schedule, you can also ask to speak with your boss outside of this schedule.

KNOW YOUR ACHIEVEMENTS

Make sure you come to your performance review meetings prepared to discuss your achievements and the work that you have delivered since your last review. If you haven't already, refer back to the 'How to track your accomplishments' section on page 141 and start tracking all the positive feedback you receive and your work wins. Measure these performance outcomes against the goals that you previously set with your boss.

ASK FOR FEEDBACK

Ask for any additional feedback or clarification on the feedback you have already received from any colleagues or directly from your boss. Be open minded when having this discussion, and be willing to accept constructive criticism so you can improve and grow in your role.

DISCUSS ANY BARRIERS OR OPPORTUNITIES

Use this discussion to identify learning and development barriers or opportunities that your boss can address or provide. If you are overloaded with a particular project or task, this may be affecting your ability to develop your skills in the role. Ask about any opportunities to get involved in a project you are interested in, provide a new service to existing clients or sign up to a course or external education program that would benefit you in your role.

COMMUNICATE YOUR REQUIREMENTS

A performance review is not only to discuss your job performance, but also for you to communicate your requirements to your boss to help you achieve your performance goals. This may include asking for an opportunity to work on a new client project, being given new responsibilities or requesting that management provides additional resource support.

RESET YOUR GOALS

At the end of the review, be sure to reset your goals for the next performance review and agree with your boss on how you will work towards achieving these goals together.

LANDING A PROMOTION OR PAY RISE

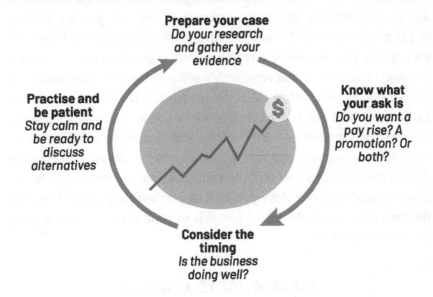

Prepare your case
Do your research and gather your evidence

Know what your ask is
Do you want a pay rise? A promotion? Or both?

Consider the timing
Is the business doing well?

Practise and be patient
Stay calm and be ready to discuss alternatives

You've worked hard, hit all your targets and received lots of positive feedback from your team and clients. It's time to get that pay rise and/or promotion you deserve.

Asking for a pay rise or promotion is incredibly nerve-racking, but there are a range of proven strategies that you can implement to successfully convince your boss that you are a unique asset to the team. It's all about preparing your case, getting specific with what you are asking for and scheduling the best time to make it happen.

PREPARE YOUR CASE

Asking for a pay rise or promotion is all about preparation. The more evidence and facts you can present to back up your case, the stronger it will be. If you haven't already, refer back to the 'How to track your accomplishments' section on page 142 and start tracking all the positive feedback you receive and your work wins. This document is the evidence you will present to your boss to justify your request.

If applicable, review your performance against your position description and also against the position description of the role you are looking to get promoted to as further justification for your request. If you are asking for a pay rise, make sure you do your research to determine what the market rate is for someone with similar skills and experience in a similar role as you. Utilise online tools such as Glassdoor, Payscale and LinkedIn Salary, and talk to any friends or contacts in your industry to determine the market rate. You will be able to use this as a benchmark when negotiating your pay rise. In addition to the above, also consider the unique value that you bring to your team and the company. Do you have a unique skill set? Have you built rapport with key clients? Are you the top performer in the team? Use this to your advantage when going into the negotiation.

KNOW WHAT YOUR ASK IS

Do you want a pay rise? Do you want a promotion? Or do you want both? Be super clear on exactly what you want before talking to your boss. Use your research to determine the precise salary increase or promotion you are requesting.

CONSIDER THE TIMING

Not only is preparation key when asking for a pay rise or promotion, but so is timing. Firstly, consider how the business has been going. If the company has had its highest year of growth and sales, then you will be in a better position to negotiate than if the business has been struggling. In addition, consider whether it is a good time for your boss. Never spring the conversation randomly on your boss or when they have back-to-back meetings. Schedule time in their calendar and preface that you want to discuss your salary/role so they are not caught off guard.

PRACTISE AND BE PATIENT

Asking for a pay rise or promotion can be scary. Practise your script beforehand so you are less nervous for the real thing. And remember to stay calm and patient. Refer back to your evidence, and if your boss can't give you exactly what you're asking for, be ready to negotiate alternatives. For example, if there's no budget for a pay rise, can you negotiate other benefits, like paid professional development or increased flexibility?

NEGOTIATING A PAY RISE/PROMOTION SCRIPT

Below is a sample script that you can use when going for a pay rise or promotion. Tweak the script where necessary to suit your personal situation.

Introduction

Thank you for taking the time to sit down with me and talk about my recent performance and career development. I want to discuss my current role and responsibilities, and how I see myself growing within the business.

Present your case

As you are aware, I've been working hard to deliver [INSERT KEY ACHIEVEMENTS/KPIS/PROJECTS] and have assisted the team with [ADDITIONAL WORK ABOVE/OUTSIDE YOUR ROLE] to make sure we are collectively achieving the company's goals. I have been able to achieve the goals that we set for me this year, which included [INSERT QUANTITATIVE GOALS AND HOW THESE WERE ACHIEVED].

Option A: Salary increase

I would like my salary to reflect the growth I have had in this role and the contributions that I am making to the company. In doing research on the salaries in the industry and the role, based on people with similar responsibilities and experience, I've found that an annual salary of [INSERT SALARY FIGURE THAT IS SLIGHTER ABOVE YOUR DESIRED

(continued)

SALARY TO ALLOW ROOM FOR NEGOTIATION] is in line with what I would like to request today.

Option B: Promotion

I would like to be considered for a promotion to [INSERT JOB TITLE] to reflect the increased responsibilities I have absorbed and the contributions I am making to the company through my work. During my time in my current role, I have been able to demonstrate my performance of the duties and responsibilities at the [INSERT JOB TITLE] level.

Closing

Thank you for your consideration. I'm looking forward to continuing working with the team to achieve successful outcomes and progressing my career journey with [INSERT COMPANY NAME].

9

Side hustles

BENEFITS OF A SIDE HUSTLE

- Boost your income
- Have an exit strategy
- Explore your interests
- Make a career shift
- Develop new skills
- Find a creative outlet

A side hustle is a form of additional income from a job you complete outside your main employment. There are a variety of benefits and reasons why you may want to start a side hustle.

BOOST YOUR INCOME

One of the most popular reasons for starting a side hustle is to increase your income. An extra $100 a week adds up to $5200 a year, and if your side hustle brings in $500 each week, that adds up to a cool $26000 a year.

No matter how much money your side hustle brings in each week, it is definitely a boost to your bank account at the end of the year. Starting a side hustle can help you boost your savings, pay off debt faster, build your emergency fund, increase your investments and hit your money goals faster.

HAVE AN EXIT STRATEGY

Another reason why you may want to start a side hustle is to create a pathway out of your current job and into self-employment. Instead of diving straight into running your own business, building it up on the side allows you to maintain your regular pay cheque and create a level of consistency and stability so you feel comfortable making the transition. How do you know when it's the right time to take your side hustle full time? It'll be different for everyone, but having an emergency fund consisting of three to six months of your living expenses will help keep your mind at ease.

EXPLORE YOUR INTERESTS

If you are not quite sure what you want to do with your career, a side hustle is a great way to explore your interests, test out different things and figure out your next step. Make a list of all your interests and think of side hustles that may align with those interests. This is a low-risk way to find out exactly what you're passionate about.

MAKE A CAREER SHIFT

Changing industries or fields is hard, especially when you don't have any experience. Starting a side hustle can help you build up this experience to add to your resumé and make the shift. Think of it as creating your own work experience job to prepare you for the next big career step.

DEVELOP NEW SKILLS

Starting a side hustle also allows you to expand your knowledge, upskill and learn new things. If you want to grow your writing skills, offer blog-writing services to businesses. If you want to get better with Excel data management, offer Excel database cleaning services to businesses. To help get started, ask your family and friends if they would be interested in you providing your services and skills.

FIND A CREATIVE OUTLET

Finding ways to monetise certain hobbies is a great way to do what you love and make money while doing so. For example, if you love fitness, you could teach group exercise classes on weekends. Or if you love painting, you could create an online store to sell your artwork.

STARTING A SIDE HUSTLE

1. Choose your perfect side hustle

2. Create your business plan

3. Schedule time to work on it

4. Market your side hustle

5. Keep track of your finances

6. Overcome any challenges

Over the next few pages, we will work through the six steps to follow to launch your side hustle. Not every step will be relevant for your side hustle, so adapt and apply any of the tips to suit you.

COMMUNITY STORY
Making the most of your skills in your side hustle

My workplace turned toxic, and it turned toxic quickly. I only had two weeks before I realised what a bad situation I was in and resigned. This was heart wrenching for me as I honestly loved my job. I'm in an in-demand industry, so finding another job was not an issue, and I had a few offers just by cold-calling places I knew I wanted to work at and reaching out through friends.

Over the past few years, I had been running a side hustle to make money outside of my 9-5. I tried different things, like selling baby blankets or doing online surveys, but needing to quit my job opened my eyes to the fact that I was utilising my 9-5 skills outside my 9-5. I had offers to work casually for a university marking papers as a side hustle, as well as contracting for other businesses for a more competitive rate.

It's been three months of working in my new roles and I am loving every minute of it. I would not have been able to even consider this without going through the trauma of leaving my previous role unexpectedly. The Smart Women Society Side Hustles 101 Game Plan bundle has been great for helping me navigate all my side hustles, making sure I set up my accounts so that I'm invoicing appropriately and putting enough aside for tax time etc.

I hope this helps someone who might be going through a rough time. University marking has been so much fun, and contracting on the side is nice as I can say 'yes' to the work that I'm super passionate about, and say 'no' to what isn't going to work for me.

Ness

CHOOSING A SIDE HUSTLE

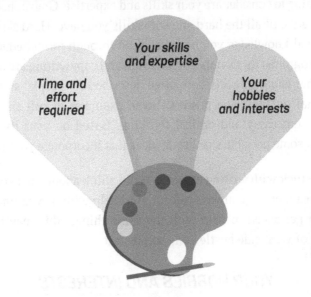

If you want to start a side hustle, the first step is choosing one that best suits your interests and lifestyle. Here are three factors to consider.

TIME AND EFFORT REQUIRED

A great place to start when determining what side hustle to pursue is deciding how much time and effort you want to commit to it. Below are some examples of low-, medium- and high-effort side hustles.

- Low-effort side hustles: online surveys, user testing
- Medium-effort side hustles: dog walking, re-selling items, food delivery
- High-effort side hustles: starting an e-commerce store, freelancing, content creator

Generally speaking, the higher the effort required, the greater the potential reward and income may be.

YOUR SKILLS AND EXPERTISE

Another thing to consider are your skills and expertise. Grab a sheet of paper and make a list of all the hard and soft skills you have. Hard skills refer to the technical knowledge you have acquired through formal education and training programs; for example, web design and copywriting are hard skills. On the other hand, soft skills are often described as 'people' skills and are the personal qualities you possess. Some examples of soft skills include leadership, creativity and critical thinking. Based on your list of skills, brainstorm some possible side hustle ideas that incorporate your skills.

If you get stuck with writing out your skills, think about what your friends and your team at work always ask for your help with. If you find that you repeatedly get asked to help with the same things, this may be a good indication of what side hustle you should start.

YOUR HOBBIES AND INTERESTS

Lastly, consider any hobbies or interests you have. Are there any that you can monetise or translate into a side hustle? You will be spending a large portion of your free time working on your side hustle, so it is beneficial to choose something you enjoy doing.

SIDE HUSTLE IDEAS

Below are 50+ side hustle ideas to get you started.

E-commerce store	Tutoring	Online surveys	Pet sitting
Social media management	Copywriting	Photography	Styling
	Coaching	Food delivery	Web design
User testing	Virtual assistant	Fitness instruction	Event planning
Dog walking	Content creation		

Exam invigilation	Mystery shopping	Personal training	Cleaning
			Blog writing
Sell on Etsy	Translation	Video editing	Sport referee/ umpire
House organisation	House sitting	Tour guide	
	Videography	DJ	Exam paper marking
Podcasting			
Interior decorating	Affiliate sales and marketing	Calligraphy	Painting
		Gardening	
Uber driving	Course creation		Pet training
	Craft/sewing	Sell on Amazon	Musician
Advertising specialist	Rent your car out	Bookkeeping	Babysitting
Resumé writing	Dropshipping	Teach a language	Data entry

MAKE A BUSINESS PLAN

- *What is your side hustle name?*
- *What makes you unique?*
- *What are your goals/objectives?*
- *Who are your main competitors?*
- *How can you do things better/differently?*
- *What problem are you aiming to solve?*
- *Who is your ideal customer?*
- *How much will your product/service cost?*

After you have chosen your perfect side hustle, spend some time working through these questions to help you define what you want to achieve with your side hustle, how your offering is unique and who you aim to serve with your product or service.

Be as detailed as possible when answering each question. For example, when defining your ideal customer, think about their age, goals, occupation, relationship status, dreams, hobbies, education, challenges and values.

Any good business or side hustle should solve a problem for their ideal customer. People should want to come to you because you have the solution to their problem/pain points. Research your ideal customer's pain points. Search for common questions in Facebook groups and other online forums that talk about your specific focus. Pay attention to what people are saying and read between the lines — the better you can help people solve their problems, the more successful your side hustle will be.

These questions will help you gain clarity on your side hustle and can be referred back to throughout your journey.

MANAGE YOUR TIME

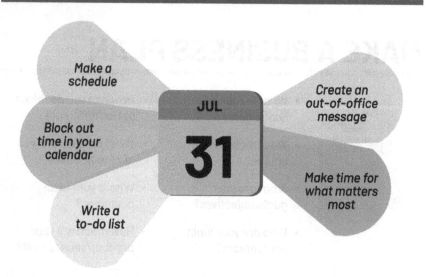

Make a schedule

Create an out-of-office message

Block out time in your calendar

JUL

31

Write a to-do list

Make time for what matters most

Managing your time effectively when you have a side hustle is crucial, or you risk burning yourself out.

MAKE A SCHEDULE

Determine how many hours and days you will commit to your side hustle. Will you only work on your side hustle on weekends? Will you dedicate a few hours every night after work? Pick your schedule and stick to it — and make sure you tell your side hustle clients or customers when your 'office hours' will be to avoid out-of-hours distractions.

BLOCK OUT TIME IN YOUR CALENDAR

Schedule your working time in your calendar to keep yourself accountable. Treat this like any other meeting or appointment, and avoid booking in any other activities during these times.

WRITE A TO-DO LIST

List out all the tasks you want and need to get done. Break down big tasks into smaller chunks and focus on completing one step at a time.

CREATE AN OUT-OF-OFFICE MESSAGE

If you plan to be away for a weekend or have a special occasion, set an out-of-office message for any side hustle communications to avoid being stuck to your email in case a client/customer reaches out.

MAKE TIME FOR WHAT MATTERS MOST

Working on your side hustle is important, but don't forget to also make time for what matters most: self-care, rest, downtime and spending time with friends and family.

MARKETING YOUR SIDE HUSTLE

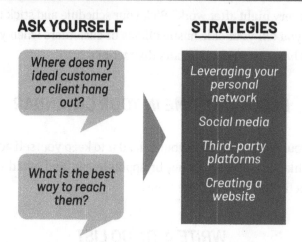

ASK YOURSELF

Where does my ideal customer or client hang out?

What is the best way to reach them?

STRATEGIES

Leveraging your personal network

Social media

Third-party platforms

Creating a website

Marketing is undoubtedly one of the hardest parts of any side hustle. You may have an amazing and unique offering, but you need to get your name out there and start making some sales. The best place to start is by asking yourself where your ideal customer or client hangs out and what is the best way of reaching them. Your time and resources are limited, so you want to be strategic with your marketing tactics.

There is no hard and fast rule for what specific marketing strategies will work for you and your side hustle. Once you understand your ideal customer or client, it is all about testing a variety of strategies and being persistent.

YOUR PERSONAL NETWORK

Your personal network is the best place to start to let people know that you are in business and to find your first client/customer. The people who know you will be more willing to give you a chance when you have no experience, and it will be less intimidating to ask for a glowing testimonial and a referral. Use your personal social media accounts to announce your side hustle and spread the word. You may also choose to offer a discounted introductory rate as you get started.

SOCIAL MEDIA

In this day and age, social media is a necessity when it comes to promoting your side hustle. Not only does it help increase your exposure, but it also allows you to connect with your existing and potential customers and clients on a much deeper level than ever before. Look back on your answers to the questions from your business plan on page 155 — what social media platforms does your ideal customer or client use? A younger target audience is likely on TikTok, whereas if you are targeting mid-career professionals, you would have better luck on LinkedIn.

Start with one or two platforms and learn how to use them well before incorporating another platform. It is better to use one platform strongly than spread yourself too thin across multiple. There are three main ways to help you gain followers, increase brand recognition and make sales fast: content, engagement and collaboration.

CONTENT

Consistency and creating valuable content are the two most important parts of your social media game. Social media can often be the last thing on your mind, so get organised by planning, creating and scheduling your content ahead of time to avoid feeling overwhelmed. If you have no idea what exactly to post, follow the 80/20 rule: 80 per cent of your content should educate, inform, inspire or entertain; the other 20 per cent should be used to sell. And lastly, but also most importantly, be unique and have fun. People relate to other people, so be yourself and show off your personality.

ENGAGEMENT

The main purpose of social media is to be social. Engage with your audience and similar accounts to help you build authentic relationships. Keep talking to your customers to learn more about their needs and get to know them better. Ask them what made them decide to buy your products or services and if anything caused them trouble or concern. You can use this feedback to update and refine your side hustle.

COLLABORATION

Collaborating with others running similar or related side hustles to yours exposes you to new audiences and allows your followers to see new perspectives. Be friendly and build authentic relationships with others. You may want to collaborate to produce content, do a giveaway or share information with your audiences.

THIRD-PARTY PLATFORMS

Another way to expose your side hustle to a wider audience is to utilise third-party platforms and websites that already have an existing audience. Here are some suggestions for both product-based and service-based side hustles.

PRODUCT-BASED SIDE HUSTLES

- Amazon is a trusted platform that can give you exposure to a very large audience, however, it can be difficult to stand out and rank among the many other products.

- Similar to Amazon, eBay is a large marketplace, however, be wary of higher selling fees.

- Etsy caters to a more niche market than Amazon and eBay, and is known for its low fees and ease of use.

- Facebook Marketplace's primary focus is buying and selling local goods.

SERVICE-BASED SIDE HUSTLES

- Freelance job boards: Sites like Fiverr, Upwork and Freelancer allow you to apply for 'jobs' posted by other users. Although this is the most straightforward way to find clients, the competition is high and payments can be low.

- Facebook groups: Join industry-related and general business groups on Facebook. Regularly scan groups and apply as soon as an interesting job shows up, or put yourself out there and post what you have to offer and that you are looking for new clients.

- Cold emailing: This one can be scary, but cold emails can also be the most effective way of getting high-paying clients. Research and find potential clients and link your website in your email. You might only receive a few replies, but those may develop into some incredible collaborations.

CREATING A WEBSITE

Even if your side hustle is done locally or you sell through a bigger third-party platform like the ones listed here, it is still a good idea to create a website for your side hustle. A website legitimises your side hustle and hosts all the information that your potential customers or clients need to know about you and your offer. Here are some of the elements that you may want to include on your website:

- About page
- What you offer
- High-quality photography
- Online store
- Portfolio/project gallery
- Current/past clients
- Testimonials
- Blog
- Terms and conditions
- Privacy policy
- Press/media page
- Contact form.

There are many websites, like WIX, Shopify or Squarespace, that make DIYing your own website simple, or you can hire a professional website developer to make one for you.

IN PERSON

Your side hustle may be best seen in person. Head down to your local community markets, take to the streets or head to the next relevant industry event and start spreading the word about what you do.

SIDE-HUSTLE FINANCES

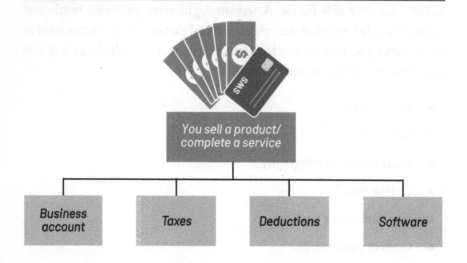

So you're making money from your side hustle — yay! But before you get too excited and spend it all, make sure your business finances are in order and you are keeping taxes in mind. For more personalised information, speak to an accountant about the financial and tax implications of your specific side hustle.

SEPARATE BUSINESS ACCOUNT

Set up a separate bank account to keep track of your side hustle income and expenses. This will allow you to never confuse your personal and side-hustle money and will simplify everything for tax season. Remember to also keep all invoices and receipts from any expenses you make during the year.

TAXES

When you receive your side-hustle income, it is likely that you will not have already paid taxes on this money. Make sure to keep a portion of this money aside for taxes (aim for at least 30 per cent) and declare all income earned from your side hustle on your tax return. You may also have to pay goods and services tax (GST) and/or sales tax depending on how much you make and where you live.

DEDUCTIONS

Make sure you know what expenses you can claim deductions for to decrease your tax payable. Generally, anything you spend that relates to you making your side-hustle income will be deductible. This means if you buy a new camera for your photography side hustle, you can claim this as a tax deduction. For more details, check out your relevant tax authority, such as the ATO.

ACCOUNTING SOFTWARE

Keep track of all your income and expenses using a bookkeeping program like Xero, MYOB or Wave. There are many options out there, so do your research and pick one that works best for you and your side hustle. While using accounting software is not compulsory, it will definitely make your life easier.

SIDE-HUSTLE CHALLENGES

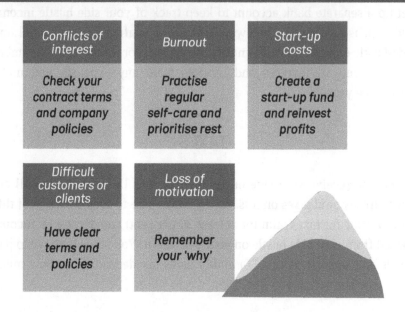

Conflicts of interest	Burnout	Start-up costs
Check your contract terms and company policies	Practise regular self-care and prioritise rest	Create a start-up fund and reinvest profits

Difficult customers or clients	Loss of motivation
Have clear terms and policies	Remember your 'why'

Having a side hustle can be incredibly rewarding, but you will undoubtedly come across various challenges. Here are five of the most common roadblocks you may face and tips on how to overcome them.

CONFLICTS OF INTEREST

Your employer may restrict your ability to have a side hustle if it is in direct competition with the work you already do for them, or if your side hustle involves a competing company. For example, if you work for a marketing agency and you want to do marketing consulting on the side, that may be a violation of your company's policies.

The contract that you signed when you were hired may also include a 'non-compete' clause that states that you will not go into competition with your employer during or after employment.

Double check your company's policies and the terms in your contract to make sure that your full-time job does not have any strict rules in place regarding side hustles. If you're in doubt, you can also speak to your HR department or manager.

Even if no conflicts of interest exist, make sure you stay productive at your main job. Don't start missing deadlines or drop the quality of your work because you are distracted by your side hustle.

BURNOUT

Starting your own side hustle can be hard enough as it is, but facing the constant challenge of fitting it in between your full-time work and daily life activities can be exhausting. The issue of burning out when you are trying to start a side hustle is high, so it is important that you consciously manage this balance.

There are a few ways you can prevent burnout. Firstly, manage your time strictly and fit your side hustle in during your most productive working hours. Secondly, set aside time to practise regular self-care. Your health is always your top priority, so recognise when you are feeling burnt out and take a step back to rest and recharge.

START-UP COSTS

Your side hustle idea may require some initial start-up costs like buying inventory or equipment. Don't let start-up costs discourage you from starting your side hustle. Investing some money up front may be necessary so you can reap the massive rewards later. Set aside a portion of your income to go towards a 'start-up fund' and avoid going into debt unless you are confident you can repay it quickly. Reinvest your initial profits back into your side hustle to buy more equipment/materials or to undertake further upskilling so that you can keep growing into the future.

DIFFICULT CUSTOMERS OR CLIENTS

While you will have positive interactions with most of your customers or clients, it is likely that you will also encounter some difficult ones. People demanding a refund, not paying you for your services, changing the scope of work, ignoring your requests for payment ... and the list goes on. It can definitely be deflating and exhausting when you encounter these sorts of customers or clients, but there are a few ways you can manage them.

MAKE A CONTRACT

Before starting with a new client, set a clear scope of work that is agreed to by both parties. This scope of work should clearly define all deadlines and how you will deal with any extra inclusions or modifications. There are websites that have contract templates you can use as a starting point. Alternatively, you can consult with a legal professional if you want to make sure that this document adequately protects you.

HAVE CLEAR PAYMENT TERMS

Be clear on when you expect payment and define late payment fees. Avoid invoicing for the total price at the end, as clients can just avoid paying your invoice when they've already received your work.

If you do end up in a situation where your client has not paid, send friendly reminder emails the day and week after payment is due and reattach the invoice. If this fails, try and discuss with your client why they have not yet paid and reiterate your payment terms. Remain calm during this process and remind yourself that you have a legal right to payment for your work. If all else fails, consider taking legal action or engaging a debt collector to recover your payment.

REFUND POLICIES

Make sure that you have a robust refund policy in place that clearly states in what circumstances you will give a customer a refund. Check the laws in your area to make sure that your policy is in line with the relevant consumer law.

LOSS OF MOTIVATION

As you pursue your side hustle, you may go through periods where you are struggling to stay motivated and committed to it. If this is the case, remember why you started your side hustle in the first place. Was it to pay off your debts faster, to quit the job you hate or to save up for a holiday? Whatever it is, use that as motivation to stay on track.

COMMUNITY STORY
Finding resilience

I dreamed of working for a company that gave me the flexibility I needed to have work/life balance, where I could be in charge of my career trajectory and learning, and make a real difference to people around me. When I couldn't find this working for other people, I realised that I needed to create it myself.

On my own, with no background in business and no help, I registered with Foundation First, secured a lease on a property and began trying to figure out how to market myself and my services to families in my local area. I was lucky to be working in health and in a high-demand role, but it took all of my strength to beat down my imposter syndrome and back myself when I started seeing clients and developing my business model. It was a tough six months of not getting paid, paying bills and praying that the risk was going to pay off.

The breakthrough finally happened a year later. I had a growing waitlist, was beginning to secure a name as a quality paediatric service and was building great relationships with the other health professionals around me. An old colleague reached out and asked for a job. I was thrilled to be able to offer her a position as my first speech pathologist.

(continued)

It's now almost two years since I opened, and I'm on the lookout for another clinician to help manage the ever-growing list of children and families who need support. For anyone who wants to start their own business, go and do it. I was so scared to be in charge of myself, to put money into something that wasn't guaranteed and to have to believe in myself. I was terrified of problem solving, being responsible for other people and worried that I would find out that I wasn't good enough to make it happen.

What I found out, instead, is that I'm resourceful, intelligent and capable. And when you want something, you're going to make it work. You find the answers, you make relationships with other business owners and learn together, and you have an opportunity to create your dream role.

Sarah

WELLBEING

In this section:

I used to be the type of person who prided themselves on always being 'busy'. In school, I was the kid who had an extracurricular activity every day before and after school. In university, I juggled full-time studies, two part-time jobs, another two side hustles, as well as saying yes to as many social events as possible. Between attending classes, studying, working and maintaining a social life, I didn't have much downtime. I was always figuring out ways to multitask and cram as much as possible into one day. If I did have a free day, I would try to pick up another shift at one of my jobs. If I had an empty gap in my calendar, I had to fill it with something productive.

The thought of having a day, or even so much as an afternoon, off terrified me. I didn't know how to relax. If I felt tired, I told myself to keep pushing. I never gave myself a chance to take a break or rest. There was always too much to do and not enough time. I only knew how to operate at 100 per cent productivity, and anything less I viewed as a failure.

In my fourth year of university, it all started unravelling. I started getting sick constantly. As soon as I recovered from one illness, I would be struck with another. My immune system was weak. I was sent to hospital twice for exhaustion and dehydration, days before my big final exams. I was burnt out and my body couldn't handle it anymore. I refused to take a break, so my body decided to take one for me. I vividly remember the doctor in the emergency room asking about my schedule and their concerned face as I listed off my daily routine. 'Do you ever *rest*?' she asked me. 'I've never heard of that word,' I replied, trying to laugh it off. I knew things had to change.

I'm much more intentional with my time now. I've learned how to slow down, focus on one thing at a time, take breaks, say 'no' more and set boundaries. Self-care and rest are now a non-negotiable part of my daily schedule. Working yourself to burnout is not a badge of honour and it's not something to glamourise. You can't run off exhaustion. You can't be your 'best' if you're running on empty.

Doing your 'best' does not mean compromising your physical and mental health. It doesn't mean pushing yourself to breaking point. Listen to your limits. Allow yourself to step away. Resting is not a sign of weakness or laziness, nor is it a waste of time. In fact, it's an essential component in living a successful, healthy and happy life.

I've learned that I can do it all, but it doesn't have to be done all at once. Resting and taking care of yourself is productive too.

10

Self-care

OUR MENTAL WELLBEING BATTERY

Let's think about our mental wellbeing as a battery. In order to keep our minds and bodies healthy, we want to make sure that our battery stays as fully charged as possible. Every week, we experience and do things that both drain our batteries and energise our batteries.

In the image on the next page, the activities on the left are some examples of what may drain you. This can include a range of things, such as being burnt out, going through a break-up, toxic friendships, health issues and feelings of stress and anxiety. On the other hand, the activities on the right are some examples of what may energise you. This can include self-care, taking the time to rest, practising regular gratitude and investing in yourself.

Think about an average week in your life. Do you feel like you're always running on zero? Are you always counting down the days to the weekend only to feel too exhausted and unmotivated to do anything? If your week is filled with activities, experiences and feelings that drain your mental wellbeing battery, you are going to feel constantly depleted and defeated.

WHAT DRAINS US	WHAT ENERGISES US

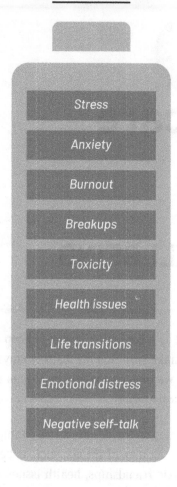

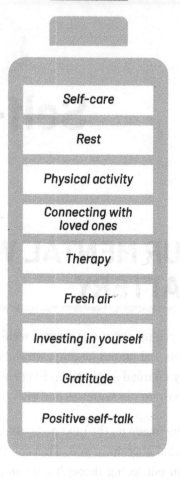

The good news is your battery can be re-charged. And there's two ways to do so.

Firstly, limit your exposure, where possible, to activities that drain you. Life is filled with unpredictable events and stressors, so it's impossible to completely eliminate or avoid draining activities. Instead, focus on how you can minimise these situations. Evaluate your friendships and relationships, set clear boundaries and get comfortable saying 'no' more to protect your energy.

Secondly, and more importantly, focus on recharging your battery with activities and experiences that energise you. Find the activities that replenish your mind, body and soul, and actively do these things on a daily basis.

BENEFITS OF SELF-CARE

Improved mood and energy levels

Enhanced self-esteem

Increased productivity

More to give to others

Increased self-knowledge

Improved physical health

What is self-care and what are the benefits? The concept of self-care can be simply defined as any activity or practice that you deliberately engage in on a regular basis that makes your mind, body and life happier and healthier. It's about being kind to yourself and knowing that when your resources are running low, you will step back to rest, recharge and re-energise.

Incorporating self-care into your daily routine leads to several incredible benefits such as:

- **Improved mood and energy levels:** Spending time resting and doing things you love increases your daily happiness and overall mood levels.

- **Enhanced self-esteem:** Making time for yourself and prioritising your needs sends a positive message to your subconscious that you matter.

- **Increased productivity:** Practising regular self-care helps you to recharge and avoid burnout. This allows you to stay calm, focused and prioritise your most important work to get more done.

- **The ability to give more to others:** You may have heard of the phrase 'you can't pour from an empty cup'. Self-care ensures that you have the resources to look after yourself and be compassionate to others.

- **Increased self-knowledge:** Self-care requires you to get to know yourself better and think about what you really love to do. What motivates and inspires you is completely different from what motivates and inspires your friends or family. That's why it is important to try a range of self-care techniques and figure out what works best for you.

- **Improved physical health:** Self-care leads to many health benefits, such as lower stress levels and an improved immune system.

SELF-CARE MINDSET SHIFTS

INSTEAD OF ...	TRY ...
Self-care is selfish.	Self-care is essential. I prioritise taking care of myself because I know I can't pour from an empty cup.
I'm too busy. I don't have time for self-care.	I will make time for self-care because I know it will nourish me physically and mentally.
Self-care is too expensive.	There are many ways that I can practise self-care daily that are free or inexpensive.
I don't know how to practise self-care.	I am experimenting and learning about the best forms of self-care for me.

If you ask someone why they don't practise regular self-care, their answer usually falls under one of the following responses:

Work is crazy right now.

My budget is tight at the moment.

I'll start next week after X, Y and Z.

I feel way too guilty to do that.

I hate bubble baths.

All of these responses perpetuate the idea that self-care is time-consuming, expensive, indulgent or selfish. But this is simply not true. You can spend as little as a few minutes a day doing something you love. There are numerous free self-care options, and it is an essential activity to help you rest, re-energise and re-connect.

Don't let these self-care myths get in the way of you getting started. Self-care should be a daily practice, not an emergency procedure. If you don't make time to look after yourself, your body will pick a time where it forces you to do so. And usually, it's not at a very convenient time. Remember, your physical and mental health is the most important thing in your life. Look after them.

The figure on the previous page lists some common excuses that people use for not practising self-care. Whenever you catch yourself thinking or saying any of these things, use the examples on the right to reframe your thoughts and make self-care a priority in your life.

TYPES OF SELF-CARE

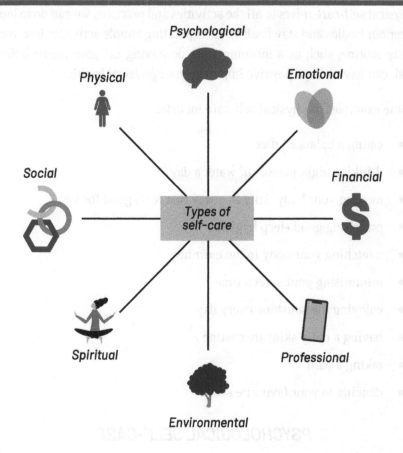

Psychological

Physical

Emotional

Social

Financial

Types of
self-care

Spiritual

Professional

Environmental

When we think of self-care, we often think of bubble baths and face masks. While these things are great (who doesn't love a pamper session?), they don't capture the full picture.

Self-care encapsulates all aspects of your life. Your mind, your body, your work, your finances, your relationships and the world around you. Let's take a closer look at the eight different types of self-care.

PHYSICAL SELF-CARE

Physical self-care refers to all the activities and practices we can do to look after our bodies and stay healthy. Incorporating simple activities into your daily routine, such as a morning walk or staying off your phone before bed, can have a huge positive impact to your physical health.

Some examples of physical self-care include:

- eating a balanced diet
- drinking eight glasses of water a day
- moving your body daily in a way that feels good for you
- practising good sleep hygiene
- stretching your body in the morning
- minimising your screen time
- enjoying the sunshine every day
- having a daily skincare routine
- taking a bath
- dancing to your favourite songs.

PSYCHOLOGICAL SELF-CARE

Psychological self-care refers to activities and practices that make you think, learn and grow. This includes anything that stimulates your mind, grows your knowledge and allows you to engage in critical thinking.

Some examples of psychological self-care include:

- learning new things
- practising mindfulness
- journaling
- going to therapy

- learning a new language
- doing a crossword or puzzle
- setting new goals
- practising self-awareness
- taking a self-development course
- being creative.

EMOTIONAL SELF-CARE

Emotional self-care refers to activities and practices that help you connect, process and reflect on your emotions. It's about getting in touch with all your feelings, whether they be good or bad, and developing strategies to help you navigate them.

Some examples of emotional self-care include:

- practising gratitude
- repeating personal affirmations
- tracking your mood
- managing stress
- going on a date
- cuddling your pet
- laughing
- setting boundaries
- spending time with yourself
- increasing your empathy.

FINANCIAL SELF-CARE

Financial self-care refers to activities and practices that allow you to feel in control of your finances. It's about being responsible with your money and developing a mindful values approach to your finances.

Some examples of financial self-care include:

- paying off debt
- creating a budget
- living within your means
- setting aside money in case of emergencies
- mindful spending
- defining your money values
- saying 'no' to things outside of your budget
- negotiating a higher salary
- protecting and insuring your assets (including yourself)
- investing for your future.

PROFESSIONAL SELF-CARE

Professional self-care refers to activities and practices that promote a healthy work-life balance and career fulfilment. It involves setting clear boundaries, taking regular breaks and pursuing a career aligned with your values and purpose.

Some examples of professional self-care include:

- developing your skills
- sharing your talents
- setting clear work boundaries
- taking your lunch break
- finding a mentor
- saying 'no'
- tracking and celebrating your accomplishments
- using your annual and sick leave

- finding a job that aligns with your career values and purpose
- planning your next career move.

COMMUNITY STORY
You don't need to do everything

I struggle with saying no to tasks at work and to people in general, so I am no stranger to having a full plate and drowning in it. I read a quote on the SWS Instagram page that said, 'I can do anything, but I cannot do everything', and it *immediately* reminded me that it's okay. Okay to not overfill my plate, okay to say 'no' to take time for myself and okay to not do everything — not because I can't, but because I don't need to spread myself so thin. I am better when I am not spread thin.

Nicola

ENVIRONMENTAL SELF-CARE

Environmental self-care refers to activities and practices that allow you to create a clean, organised and motivating environment, both at work and at home. This not only involves your physical space, but also encompasses activities to minimise waste and reduce screen time.

Some examples of environmental self-care include:

- de-cluttering your wardrobe
- having a clean and safe living environment
- decorating your home/workspace
- exploring a new area
- minimising waste
- opening all the windows in your home and letting the fresh air come in
- re-arranging furniture around your home

- watering your plants
- monitoring technology time
- switching up your workspace for the day.

SOCIAL SELF-CARE

Social self-care refers to activities and practices that help you nurture and deepen your relationships with others. The types of social self-care activities that you enjoy will vary depending on whether you are an extrovert or introvert, but regardless, they will help you build trust and strengthen your friendships and relationships. Nurturing your relationships with the important people in your life helps you feel more connected and leads to an increased sense of belonging.

Some examples of social self-care include:

- having supportive and caring people around you who you can trust
- asking for help
- spending quality time with loved ones
- having a date night with your partner
- catching up with a friend you haven't seen in a while
- unfollowing negative people on social media
- joining a club/group (e.g. social sport, book club)
- setting boundaries
- meeting new people
- calling your parents or grandparents.

SPIRITUAL SELF-CARE

Spiritual self-care refers to activities and practices that nurture your spirit and sense of connection. It involves the beliefs and values that are important to you and underpin your life, as well as any things that make your heart or soul flourish. This does not necessarily need to involve religion, but it may for some.

Some examples of spiritual self-care include:

- meditating
- setting goals
- reflecting
- watching the sunset
- being part of a community
- doing yoga
- volunteering
- being in nature
- donating to a charity
- advocating for a cause you believe in.

Incorporating many different types of self-care will ensure that you are looking after all aspects of your mind, body and soul. It is important to note, however, that self-care will look different for everyone. There are many ways to practise self-care. Every single person will enjoy (and not enjoy) different things.

Once you have read through all the examples of self-care activities, spend some time testing out the ones that stood out to you. This will help you understand what you enjoy and what makes you feel more rested, energised and connected. Then, incorporate more of these activities into your daily routine.

The easiest way to do this is by scheduling them in your calendar and treating them like any other appointment or important meeting. For example, schedule time in your calendar for walks, de-cluttering or even short five-minute activities — and stick to it. By doing so, you are making a commitment to yourself to prioritise your mental wellbeing.

BOOSTING YOUR DAILY HAPPINESS

Make a list of what **makes you happy**

Make a list of what **you do every day**

Compare the lists. Adjust accordingly.

We often get so consumed in the never-ending to-dos and busy-ness of life that we never take a moment to step back and evaluate our daily habits and routines. But perhaps more importantly, when was the last time you sat down and really thought about what makes you truly happy?

Grab two sheets of paper. On one sheet, write a list of everything that makes you happy. This could be anything from buying yourself fresh flowers from the markets to lying on the couch eating ice cream and watching *Love Island*. Whatever it is, be as specific as possible. Think about the people you're around, where you are and what you're doing.

On the second sheet of paper, write a list of things you do daily. What does a typical weekday and weekend day look like for you?

Once you've written the two lists, it's time to compare them and adjust your habits and routines accordingly.

How does it look? Are you incorporating things that make you happy into your everyday routine?

Can you change the way you start your morning?

Is there anything you can alter in your night-time routine?

What daily habits can you work on that focus on your happiness?

What do you want to do more of? What do you want to do less of?

Make adjustments where you can. Start small — doing more of just one thing will have a huge impact on your overall happiness.

STARTING YOUR MORNING

- *One accomplishment you are proud of from yesterday*

- *One thing you are looking forward to today*

- *Five people in your life you are thankful for*

- *One thing you like about the way you look*

- *Your intention for the day*

And five deep breaths!

The first hour of your morning sets the tone for the rest of the day. Start your day on a positive note by answering these five points. It doesn't matter how you answer them: in your head while lying in bed, out loud in the mirror or in a notebook. Do whatever works best for you. What's important is that you take a moment to reflect, be present and practise some self-love and gratitude. Finish off with five big, deep breaths to calm your body and release any stress or tension. Make this activity a regular part of your morning routine and you'll notice a huge difference to your day.

HOW TO SLEEP BETTER

- Don't watch the clock: if you can't sleep, get back up
- Stop using screens one hour before bed
- Try not to nap during the day
- Make the room dark, quiet and cool
- Have a bedtime routine (e.g. reading, meditation)
- Have regular sleep and waking times
- Put your phone on silent and out of reach
- Minimise caffeine in the afternoon and evenings

If only getting a good night's sleep was as easy as shutting your eyes and waking up feeling refreshed and ready to take on the day. In reality, many of us experience restless nights of tossing and turning in our beds. Sleep affects so many things, including our:

- mood
- memory
- stress levels
- decision-making ability

- immune system
- skin
- creativity.

Keeping a sleep diary allows you to keep track of any patterns in your sleep and your mood the following day. Some things you can track in your sleep diary include:

- What time did you get into bed?
- What time did you try and sleep?
- Did anything prevent you from falling asleep (e.g. noise, anxious thoughts)?
- How many times did you wake up during the night?
- Did anything disturb your sleep?
- What time did you wake up in the morning?
- What mood were you in when you woke up and throughout the following day?

Follow the tips in the figure on page 188 for a better night's sleep. If you are having ongoing sleep problems, speak with a medical professional.

11
Burnout

SIGNS OF BURNOUT

EXHAUSTION
- Physical, emotional and mental exhaustion
- Always mentally 'on' and unable to relax
- Difficulty motivating yourself to get out of bed or to work
- Feeling over-extended and time pressured
- Having an intense daily schedule and workload

NEGATIVITY
- Distancing yourself mentally from people or work
- Not engaging with friends, family, colleagues or clients
- Feelings of indifference, detachment and/or cynicism
- Being surrounded by conflict or unfairness
- Lack of participation in decision making

SELF-BELIEF
- Lack of support from the people around you
- Not having clear goals you are working towards
- Feeling like you are not accomplishing anything
- Absence of meaningful recognition and appreciation
- Inadequate resources, such as time or information

Burnout is more than just feeling stressed. It presents itself as physical and mental exhaustion, a growth in negativity about our lives, and a reduction in our confidence and self-belief in the path we are on. It's our body's way of telling us that we've reached our limit and we need to rest. It is important you keep an eye out for any of the warning signs that you may be burnt out. Identifying which signs you see in your own life will help you manage and overcome the burnout.

COMMUNITY STORY
Finding balance, not burnout

I work full time while also trying to finish my degree online. The whole work/study balance is enough to consume a lot of my energy, but keeping on top of my own health, finances and relationships has been a challenge as well. When I put all of my energy into work, my study slides. When I fall behind on my study, stress becomes a problem. When I'm stressed, my health takes a hit, and I can't be there for my relationships or be my best at work.

There's a lot of pressure to 'do your best', 'hustle' and 'give 110%', but the other side of this is ending up depleted and burnt out. I'm still learning, but I have started to set boundaries and limits for each of these different sections of my life, and am being patient with myself. It's okay to take a break or rest. Actually, it's good for you. You can't be 'on' 24/7.

Christina

EFFECTS OF BURNOUT

Lack of enthusiasm

Decreased productivity and output of work

Difficulty sleeping

Constant exhaustion

Making mistakes more often

Neglecting personal care, needs and important commitments

Prolonged negative attitude and /or cynicism

Vulnerability to illness

Feeling frustrated, overwhelmed and anxious

Low job satisfaction and employer loyalty

Headaches and other physical side effects

Reduced creativity

Burnout can have prolonged and severe effects on your physical and mental wellbeing. While the effects will be different for everyone, burnout typically negatively impacts your mood, energy levels and productivity. Burnout can also directly impact the people around you, putting strain on your relationships with your friends, family and co-workers. During periods of burnout, we are unable to perform at our best and all aspects of our lives begin to suffer.

MANAGING BURNOUT

- Schedule appointments with yourself in your calendar for rest and to do things you enjoy

- Set and enforce boundaries around the activities/people that are contributing to your burnout the most

- Ensure you are getting enough sleep, rest and regular exercise

- Recognise what you can vs what you can't control

- Spend more time with people who you feel your most authentic self around

- Limit interactions with people who are negative or bring you down

- Find a new hobby or get involved in a community/social group that interests you

- Re-evaluate your personal and career values and assess whether your current job and habits aligns with them

- Allocate a technology-free time of the day to unwind and calm your mind

Managing and overcoming burnout isn't always straightforward. As it is often caused by a combination of factors, recovery from burnout is also an incremental process and requires change across various parts of your life. The figure here includes some examples of ways to manage and overcome burnout. It is important to first understand the root causes of your burnout (e.g. struggling to say no at work) and then adopt strategies and habits that directly target these causes.

No matter what specific activities you choose to implement, the most crucial aspect is ensuring that you stick to them consistently over a period of time. A weekend away is not going to fix your burnout if you are going back to the same routine and environment that put you there in the first place. As always, set your goals and keep yourself accountable for putting your burnout recovery plan into place.

HOW TO LEAVE WORK STRESS AT WORK

- *Clear your space*
- *Plan out tomorrow*
- *Transition out of work mode*
- *Set boundaries*
- *Switch off*

Your work day doesn't end when you walk out the door or shut down your computer if you continue to stress and think about all of the issues, irritations and activities you need to do the next day. Our minds are unable to get the rest they need if you don't switch off and disconnect from work. Even if you are not physically doing work-related activities outside of work hours, it's important to implement boundaries and strategies to help you leave work stress at work at the end of the day.

CLEAR YOUR SPACE

Take a few minutes at the end of your workday to clear your desk or workspace. Put away any papers, take your mug to the sink and wipe down any dust or dirt. Not only does this signal to your brain that you have packed up for the day, but there is also no better feeling than coming in to a fresh workspace in the morning.

PLAN OUT TOMORROW

Before wrapping up for the day, grab a sheet of paper and brain dump everything that is on your mind. Write out any outstanding tasks, things you need to follow up, ideas, reminders and anything else you need to take action on or remember to do. Doing so will clear your mind of all work-related tasks and thoughts that may stay ruminating in your mind at night. Then, review your calendar for tomorrow and map out your day so you can hit the ground running in the morning.

TRANSITION OUT OF WORK MODE

Create a ritual that marks the transition from your work to your personal life. This could be watching a YouTube video on your train ride home, heading to the gym, changing out of your work clothes or calling or texting a friend to talk about something that isn't related to work. Whatever it is, your ritual should help you decompress after a long day and relax.

SET BOUNDARIES

Communicate openly with your manager or boss if you are feeling overwhelmed or over-extended at work. Have an honest, pragmatic conversation about your current workload and any struggles or issues you are facing. Set boundaries around working hours and avoid setting the expectation that you will respond to work calls or emails out of hours.

SWITCH OFF

Give yourself permission to log off from all forms of communication at the end of the workday. Turn off notifications to avoid seeing late-night emails, or take it a step further and delete the email app off your phone entirely. Instead, prioritise making time for your hobbies, self-care and spending time with friends and family.

TYPES OF REST

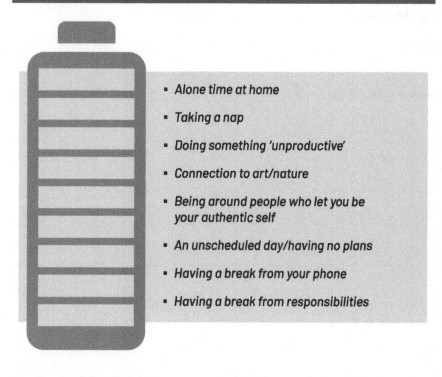

- *Alone time at home*
- *Taking a nap*
- *Doing something 'unproductive'*
- *Connection to art/nature*
- *Being around people who let you be your authentic self*
- *An unscheduled day/having no plans*
- *Having a break from your phone*
- *Having a break from responsibilities*

Resting is more than just getting into bed for a good night's sleep. Rest can be defined as anything that recharges your physical and mental wellbeing, and it comes in many different forms, such as the types listed here. Trialling and learning the best forms of rest that work for you is a key component to combating and managing burnout.

For example, if you are feeling mentally exhausted at work, take a lunch break without sitting and scrolling through social media.

If you have had a busy week studying and finishing assessments, plan a morning walk and breakfast with your best friend.

If your social battery is drained, say no to after-work drinks and put on your favourite movie at home.

Listen to your body's needs and prioritise making time to rest on a regular basis.

12

Motivation

HOW TO SET GOALS THAT YOU'LL ACTUALLY STICK TO

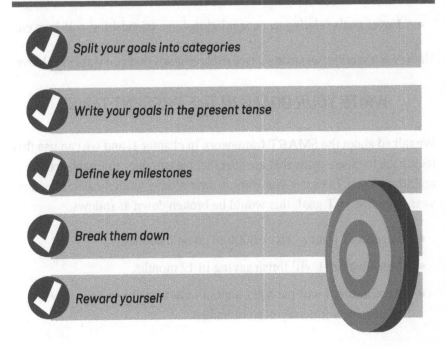

✓ Split your goals into categories

✓ Write your goals in the present tense

✓ Define key milestones

✓ Break them down

✓ Reward yourself

Setting goals gives your life direction, aligns your focus and helps you develop new behaviours and habits to become the best version of you. But do you ever wonder why we get so excited to set goals on New Year's Eve every year, then by the end of January, most people have given up on them already? That's because there's an art to setting goals that you'll actually stick to. Let's break it down.

SPLIT YOUR GOALS INTO CATEGORIES

If you have no idea where to start when setting goals, split them into categories across the various aspects of your life. Grab a sheet of paper and divide the page into four sections. Label the sections:

- **Money:** goals relating to saving, investing, budgeting, paying off debt etc.

- **Career:** goals relating to your job, getting a promotion, starting a business etc.

- **Wellbeing:** goals relating to your physical and mental health, productivity, spirituality, self-motivation etc.

- **Love:** goals relating to your relationships, friendships, self-love etc.

Under each section, write down two to three goals that you want to achieve.

WRITE YOUR GOALS IN THE PRESENT TENSE

We talked about the SMART framework in chapter 1, and we can use this technique to create goals that are specific, measurable, attainable, relevant and time-based. Let's say you want to save money to go on a holiday next year. As a SMART goal, this would be broken down as follows.

- **Specific:** I want to save $5000 to go on a holiday.

- **Measurable:** I will finish saving in 12 months.

- **Attainable:** I will put $417 a month towards my savings. This is achievable within my current budget.

- **Relevant:** Travel is something I love and deeply value. I am also looking forward to a break from work.

- **Time-based:** I will start saving on [DATE] and finish in 12 months on [DATE].

Your final SMART goal would be: I want to save $5000 in 12 months to go on a holiday. I will do this by saving $417 a month.

What's missing in the SMART goal technique, however, is a crucial step — and that's writing your goals in the present tense ('I am' or 'I have'). Writing your goals as if they have already happened helps your subconscious mind to visualise your success and reinforce that you have the ability to achieve that goal.

So, for the example above, it would be reworded as: I am so happy that I have $5000 in my savings account for my holiday.

DEFINE KEY MILESTONES

Break down your goal into key milestones; for example, if your goal is to save $5000 in 12 months, you can set a milestone to save $1250 every quarter. Setting milestones helps you to stay on track and makes your bigger goal feel more achievable. Check in with your goals regularly or ask a friend, colleague or loved one to keep you accountable. Review your progress and tweak or modify your goal if necessary.

BREAK THEM DOWN

You have written out your goal and defined key milestones, but the next step is figuring out the exact action plan you need to follow to actually achieve it. Under each milestone, write out a list of things you need to do to achieve that milestone. For example, to hit your first quarterly milestone of $1250 in savings, you may decide to sell your unworn clothes and cut back on eating out and put that into savings instead. Be specific about the tasks you need to do to progress towards your goal.

REWARD YOURSELF

Set a reward for when you achieve your goal or for when you achieve milestones along the way. Working towards a goal is no easy feat, but your hard work will pay off. The reward doesn't need to be extravagant or expensive — it can be an at-home pamper night or enjoying a nice dinner out. What is important is that it is something that gets you excited and keeps you motivated to work towards your goal.

Use this template to put the above tips into practice. You can also download a free copy at: **smartwomensociety.com/smartmoves-goalstemplate**.

CATEGORY:

GOAL:

KEY MILESTONES

Milestone 1 Milestone 2 Milestone 3 Milestone 4

TO DO

☐ _____ ☐ _____ ☐ _____ ☐ _____
☐ _____ ☐ _____ ☐ _____ ☐ _____
☐ _____ ☐ _____ ☐ _____ ☐ _____
☐ _____ ☐ _____ ☐ _____ ☐ _____
☐ _____ ☐ _____ ☐ _____ ☐ _____
☐ _____ ☐ _____ ☐ _____ ☐ _____
☐ _____ ☐ _____ ☐ _____ ☐ _____

REWARD:

COMPLETED? ☐

WHAT TO DO IF YOU FEEL STUCK IN YOUR LIFE

1. Take a step back and reflect
2. Write down your current situation
3. Re-evaluate your overall path
4. Be honest with yourself
5. List all your options and opportunities
6. Seek advice from mentors
7. Set new goals for yourself
8. Don't overthink everything: keep learning and moving forward
9. Check in and adjust your strategy
10. Stay patient and trust your journey

If you ever think to yourself 'What am I doing with my life?', you're not alone. The ups and downs of life can cause you to question your career, relationships, living situation, friendships and so much more. In these moments, take some time to complete a self-review and re-evaluation. The 10 steps outlined here will give you the best opportunity to work through this stuck feeling and give you a clear next step to progress towards.

Start off by deep diving into the exact reasons why you feel stuck in your life. Write a list of everything you do and don't like about your current situation. Be as detailed and honest as possible. Are there specific situations that bother you? Is it your work or the people in your life that are the underlying issue? Are there certain things keeping you in your current position?

Once you have laid it all out, the next step is to brainstorm your potential options and opportunities. Look at your options and weigh up the pros and cons of each. Talk to mentors and others you trust for advice, but be careful not to let their words influence your decision too much. Trust your gut. Only you truly know the best decision for you. Making a big life change is scary, but it can also be the best decision you ever make. Stop overthinking everything; keep learning, setting new goals and moving forward.

Lastly, put in the time and work. Making big plans and setting goals is great, but what's even more important is actioning them. Check in with yourself regularly along the way and adjust your strategy or approach where needed. Stay patient as you inevitably encounter setbacks and obstacles along the way. Trust your journey — it will all work out.

FIXED VS GROWTH MINDSET

FIXED	vs	GROWTH
Abilities are fixed		Abilities can grow and develop
Easily gives up when challenged		Focuses on the journey not the outcome
Compares to the success of others		Embraces new challenges
Stays in the comfort zone		Can celebrate and learn from others' mistakes
Doesn't try due to fear of failure		Likes to explore and try new things

A key to fulfilling your potential is transitioning yourself from a fixed mindset to a growth mindset. Don't underestimate the power of your mindset. This shift is often the difference between two people with the same talent and skill set, but only one achieving their goals and dreams.

A fixed mindset means that you believe your talents, abilities and intelligence are fixed. If you're not good at something, you believe you'll never be good at it. Having a fixed mindset will hold you back before you even start. The belief is that there is no changing your current position and you are not confident enough, good enough or able to overcome a challenge. A fixed mindset keeps you away from incredible opportunities as you don't have the self-confidence or self-belief to try new things without the fear of failure.

On the other hand, a growth mindset means that you believe your talents, abilities and intelligence can be improved and developed over time through learning, effort and practice. Adopting a growth mindset requires you to understand that your skills and talent can be developed by facing new challenges and by putting yourself into unfamiliar environments outside of your comfort zone. Instead of viewing failure as a setback, you view it as an essential part of growth.

DEVELOPING A GROWTH MINDSET

Look for the
good in every
situation

Learn
something
new every day

You either win or
learn; failure
does not exist

Be proud of the
person you are and
avoid comparing
yourself to others

Reframe
challenges as
opportunities

Be proactive in
going after the
things you want

Start your day
with the
hardest task

Seek feedback
from people you
respect

A growth mindset means that you are always open to learning new things and you constantly strive to be better every day. When you develop a growth mindset, you are able to see your current position as the start of your journey of personal development and lifelong learning. It's all about embracing and enjoying the journey, not just the outcome or destination. Focus on your own path and know that the only person you need to compete with is the person you were yesterday. There is no such thing as shortcuts or the 'easy route'. Be proactive and embrace the opportunities that come your way. True growth comes from a cycle of trying, failing, learning and trying again. It may not feel like it in the moment, but when you zoom out, you will be able to see just how far you've come.

VISUALISING YOUR DREAM LIFE

MY VISION BOARD

1. *Define your dream life*
2. *Create a vision board*
3. *Look at it daily*

Having a clear vision of your dream life and what you are working towards helps keep you on track when challenges and setbacks try getting in the way. Visualisation is a powerful technique we can use to control our thoughts, actions and, ultimately, the direction we are heading in.

DEFINING YOUR DREAM LIFE

To help define your dream life, ask yourself the following questions:

In my dream life...

- What does my ideal life look like?
- Where do I live?
- What do I do for work?
- Who is around me?
- What makes me happy?
- What do my bank accounts look like?
- What does my daily life look like?
- How would people describe me?
- What is my legacy?

Get really specific when answering each question. Write down all the details in the present tense, as if you are living that life right now.

VISION BOARDS

Vision boards are a tool that can be used to develop and visualise your goals. They typically contain a collage of images, words, symbols and any other physical or digital objects that represent your desires, goals and life aspirations. Your vision board becomes the physical reminder of your vision that you can use as a daily reminder of why you are doing what you do. Creating a vision board is a fun and relaxing activity to do every year (or as frequently as you like). Follow these steps to get started:

1. Scroll through Pinterest and start saving images and quotes that symbolise your goals and the energy you want to attract. Gather images to visually represent the answers to the questions on page 208.

2. Open up PowerPoint or Canva and insert all the photos (or you can print them off and create one on a poster/sheet of paper).

3. Rearrange and layer your images to create your vision board. Have fun with it and create a design that you love.

4. Once you're done, save your vision board as your computer/phone wallpaper.

Look at your vision board daily and imagine that you have already achieved or have what you are looking at. This will ensure your subconscious mind stays focused on your goals.

LIMITING VS EMPOWERING BELIEFS

LIMITING BELIEFS	VS	EMPOWERING BELIEFS
I'm scared of failing		All my past failures have helped me learn and grow
I don't know how to do it		I will invest my time in learning how to do it
I'm too old		I have all the time I need and am wiser at my current age
It's too hard		If it were easy, everyone would do it
I'm not good enough		I am worthy of this
I'm so dumb		I'm still learning
I don't have enough time		What do I want to make time for?
Why is this happening to me?		What is this teaching me?

The way you talk to yourself can completely alter the pathway of your life. Our internal dialogue has a significant impact on our perspective in life, our daily moods, our attitudes and, ultimately, whether we are on the path to growth or stagnation. An important concept to understand when it comes to our internal dialogue is the difference between limiting and empowering beliefs.

Your beliefs carry with them either positive or negative emotions and these emotions then turn into actions (or inaction). If you tell yourself repeatedly that you are not good enough, you will be unhappy and regretful, which will lead to no action. Conversely, if you tell yourself that, no matter what, you can and will achieve a particular goal, you become confident and assertive, which will lead to you taking that first step. Small changes to our internal beliefs have a huge effect on our daily lives.

LIMITING BELIEFS

To put it simply, limiting beliefs hold you back in life. They are the beliefs that make you lose confidence and not apply for that job you want, not start that business you have always dreamed of or make you question your value or abilities. These beliefs stem from our experiences in life growing up and can manifest themselves into the internal fears we face today.

It is important to reflect on where your limiting beliefs may have come from so you can effectively combat them and transition them into empowering beliefs.

Some examples of where your limiting beliefs may have developed from include:

- being told you weren't good enough by the people around you
- being reprimanded when you did something wrong or didn't live up to standards imposed on you
- your achievements never being celebrated
- hearing and accepting 'this is how it has always been' or 'this is what we do'
- experiencing a traumatic event.

Limiting beliefs are often fear-based statements ('I'm scared of...' or 'I don't know...') or 'too' statements ('I'm too old/young/inexperienced').

It is the voice in your head telling you to not even bother because you will fail anyway. These beliefs can be loud, and you may not even realise that they consume your entire internal dialogue.

EMPOWERING BELIEFS

On the other hand, empowering beliefs push you to where you want to go. Rooted in unwavering self-belief, resilience and continuous learning, they are the encouragement you need to take that first step or to push you through life's challenges. While it may be hard and you may face challenges, empowering beliefs allow you to set bigger goals and keep you motivated throughout the journey to achieving them. Empowering beliefs do not come naturally to most people, so you need to practise them consistently in your daily life, and consciously change the dialogue you are having with yourself.

DEVELOPING EMPOWERING BELIEFS

The first step to transitioning your limiting beliefs into empowering beliefs is to assess your attitude towards key aspects of your life. Think about your health, relationships, financial position, career and your future. How do you internally think about these areas of your life? Do you have a positive or negative attitude towards them?

The next step is fighting back. Take one of the limiting beliefs you have and push back on it. If you think you can't get that promotion at work, ask yourself why not? Dig deeper and determine if this is really true or if you are holding yourself back due to a past experience. Ask yourself what it would take to get that promotion. Do you need to put yourself forward more, take more opportunities or change your approach? Try this exercise for all the key aspects of your life. The deeper you assess your limiting beliefs, the clearer it becomes that they are not justified, and you can begin to make a change.

Lastly, repeat these actions consistently so they become second nature. Challenging your limiting beliefs and reframing them to be more empowering is difficult and it takes time to rewire your brain to view things differently. Be patient and remind yourself that small changes over time have a significant impact on the trajectory of your life.

HOW TO CHALLENGE NEGATIVE THOUGHTS

How likely is it that this will happen?

Is this thought coming from a limiting belief that I have?

Is it true or am I making assumptions?

Will this matter in six months, one year or five years?

What would I say to a friend if they had this thought?

What is the worst that could realistically happen?

How can I reframe this thought?

The thoughts we have every day shape the way we live and the outcomes of our lives. Our internal self-talk creates the beliefs that we live by. Persistent negative thoughts can diminish our self-esteem and lead us to form limiting beliefs about ourselves and our abilities. It is so easy to get in your head and put yourself down or misconstrue a situation that we often don't even consciously realise that we are doing it.

The next time you have a negative thought, challenge that thought by asking yourself the questions listed in the graphic above. You'll find that when you dig a little deeper, most of the negative thoughts you have are irrational and not based on real, objective facts. Adopting healthier self-talk is not an easy task, but it is a mental habit that can be developed and nurtured over time with repetition and consistent action.

WHY YOU SHOULD PUSH YOURSELF OUT OF YOUR COMFORT ZONE

PROMOTE PERSONAL GROWTH

Facing new challenges allows you to grow and boosts your self-confidence.

EXPLORE YOUR PASSIONS

Pushing yourself out of your comfort zone allows you to explore and discover your passions and interests.

YOUR COMFORT ZONE

ACQUIRE NEW SKILLS

Taking on new tasks allows you to learn new skills and develop the ones you already have further.

DISCOVER NEW OPPORTUNITIES

Trying new things exposes you to new situations and opportunities. You never know where it may lead you.

We are all creatures of habit. It's how our brains are wired. We seek comfort in our daily lives by creating habits and staying in familiar environments that we feel safe operating in. This is known as our comfort zone. While this is important, we may find ourselves feeling stuck or unmotivated as we roll through the motions. If this is the case, it may be time for you to get out of your comfort zone.

All humans require a sense of growth and adventure. Pushing yourself out of your comfort zone allows you to achieve this, as it forces you to adapt to unfamiliar situations and learn new things. Venturing out of your comfort zone also promotes personal growth, and allows you to explore your passions, acquire new skills and discover new opportunities.

HOW TO PUSH YOURSELF OUT OF YOUR COMFORT ZONE

Find a support network

Set a goal that will help you grow and take a small step towards it every day

Challenge yourself to do something that you know is hard or scary

YOUR COMFORT ZONE

Accept failure is part of the process

Change up your daily routine

Try new things/take calculated risks

You may be thinking: 'All this talk about pushing myself out of my comfort zone is great, but *how* do I actually go about doing it?' To answer your question, start small. Make conversation with someone you have never spoken to at work, try a new recipe for dinner or put your hand up to present something at your next team meeting. Challenge yourself to do things that you know are hard or scary. After a while, you'll realise that they're not as scary as you made them out to be in your head.

Keep expanding your comfort zone by trying new things and taking calculated risks. Set big goals that will help you grow and take a small step towards them every day. Find people with a similar growth mindset who are also looking for new challenges and to better themselves. You will be able to support each other on your journeys by celebrating the wins and reflecting on the losses.

And lastly, but most importantly, learn to accept that failure is a part of the process. The fear of failure holds us back every day from achieving our goals. Knowing that you will be met with setbacks and failure on the way will allow you to focus on the lesson that can be learned in that moment rather than the disappointment of the outcome.

OVERCOMING YOUR FEAR OF FAILURE

COMMON SIGNS YOU MIGHT HAVE A FEAR OF FAILURE

1. Worrying about what others think of you

2. Setting low expectations for yourself

3. Procrastinating when you face a big task or challenge

4. Holding on to your past failures

5. Not learning from your past failures

6. Not being able to accept constructive criticism or assistance

7. Always doubting your skills or ability

8. Not being able to think of different solutions to a problem

Overcoming your fear of failure is the key to unlocking your full potential and creating your dream life. While fearing failure is an inherent human trait, it is something that we can control. The traits listed here are some of the most common signs that you have a fear of failure. Reflect honestly on each point and think about whether it applies to you. Through shifting our mindset and reducing risk, we are able to re-shape what we are fearful of, how we perceive this fear, how we are impacted by the fear and how we overcome it.

SHIFT YOUR MINDSET

Shifting your mindset around failure as a whole is the most effective way to overcome your fear. To shift your mindset, you need to go deeper than your reactive emotions and thoughts. It is about changing the internal dialogue of your unconscious mind, and training yourself to view failure in a more positive light. We can alter this through the internal conversations and thoughts we have with ourselves, the media and information we expose ourselves to, the discussions we have with others and by challenging our preconceived notions towards failure.

Start by cultivating a sense of gratitude towards failure. Be thankful for all the setbacks, roadblocks and closed doors. Whenever you 'fail', it means that that path or that place or that person was not meant for you, and you are being redirected to something even better.

Failure is a step to success. If you don't fail, it means you never tried. If you try to avoid failure, you will also avoid potential success. Learn to be resilient and extract lessons from your failures. Think of ways you can improve for next time. Stop worrying about what others will think, and be proud of yourself for having the courage to try. Embrace the idea that next time you won't be starting from scratch, you'll be starting with experience. Believe whole-heartedly that failure is an opportunity to learn and grow. It is on the basis of these ideas that you will redefine what failure means to you and remove the fear aspect out of it.

REDUCE YOUR RISK

Failure is inevitable. There is no way that you can cruise through life without a setback or something going wrong. What you can do, however, is minimise the potential impact of any failures by reducing your risk and implementing a mitigation plan. Say you wanted to start a new business, but you are worried that it will fail. Your mitigation plan to reduce the risk of failure would include having a solid business plan, learning the skills you need to succeed and building an emergency fund before you start.

Another factor to consider when devising your mitigation plan is the worst-case scenario. Ask yourself: 'What is the worst that can happen?' as well as 'What is the likelihood that this will actually happen?' Be neutral and realistic when answering these questions, and objectively look at the facts of the decision or situation. Most of the time you will realise that the worst-case scenario is not that bad or, if it is, the likelihood that it will eventuate is low.

When you start to consider risk management and plan ahead for any contingencies, you will have the comfort and confidence you need to embrace a new opportunity or make a decision without the fear of failure.

HOW TO STOP DOUBTING YOURSELF

- *Increase your self-awareness*
- *Change your self-talk*
- *Surround yourself with supportive people*
- *Believe in your potential*
- *Focus on your own path*
- *Take the first step*

We are not born with self-doubt. It is something that we develop through our life experiences and the impacts of the people around us. Self-doubt is the lack of confidence and belief in ourselves and our ability. It's the voice in your head telling you that you're not good enough, that it won't work out, that someone else is better at it or that you will fail. We all experience self-doubt. Even the most successful people in the world doubt themselves. What sets them apart, though, is that they have learned ways to conquer this self-doubt, and use it instead as a powerful tool to take action.

INCREASE YOUR SELF-AWARENESS

The first step in overcoming self-doubt is to increase your self-awareness and understanding of what is holding you back. Think about the specific scenarios or situations that cause you to doubt yourself. Maybe you're scared of sharing your ideas with your team because you're worried they're not any good, or maybe you want to apply for your dream role but you don't tick 100 per cent of the boxes. Reflect on the limiting beliefs you have and how these impact your self-doubt. Once you do this, you can start to take action.

CHANGE YOUR SELF-TALK

After you identify what's holding you back, it's time to start changing your self-talk. Look back on the previous chapters in this book and challenge your negative thoughts and the reasons why you doubt yourself. Consistently challenging your self-talk will result in huge benefits over time as your subconscious mind starts to adopt new empowering beliefs and positive ways of thinking.

SURROUND YOURSELF WITH SUPPORTIVE PEOPLE

Who we surround ourselves with will have a significant effect on us. Think about the five people you spend the most time around. How do they make you feel? After spending time with them, do you feel energised and inspired or drained and grumpy? Audit your circle and spend less time around people who attract negativity and hold you back. Instead, prioritise nurturing relationships with supportive people who you can seek guidance from during the doubting times, and who will cheer you on when you need that extra push. This could be a friend, family member or a mentor. Reciprocate the positive energy and elevate this person and the people around you. Remind them of their special skills and talents and how proud you are of them.

BELIEVE IN YOUR POTENTIAL

Self-doubt often causes us to justify situations, make up excuses and think of a million reasons why we can't, won't or shouldn't do something. But when was the last time you actually believed in your own potential? Think about all your past achievements. Think about all the times you did something that felt scary or unfamiliar or impossible at the time. Sit in that feeling of overcoming your self-doubt. You've done it before, and you will do it again. Stop letting self-doubt get in the way of going after what you want and achieving your goals.

FOCUS ON YOUR OWN PATH

How many times have you compared yourself to a friend, sibling, colleague or a random person you've stalked online? It's human nature to compare ourselves to others. The difference, though, is whether we use this comparison as a form of jealousy or discomfort to fuel our self-doubt, or as a source of inspiration.

Every single person is on their own journey. We all have unique backgrounds, circumstances and varying levels of privileges. When you see someone doing well or succeeding, clap for them. Take it as motivation and inspiration to see if you can find a way to achieve it too. There is enough room in this world for us all to succeed. Find ways to learn from others' success and then focus your energy on your own unique path.

TAKE THE FIRST STEP

We all have that 'thing' we want or need to do. You already know what the 'thing' is. You're probably thinking about it right now as you read this. You've been avoiding it and putting it off for a while now. Most likely because you're scared of taking the first step. But here's your reminder that you are brave. Go do the thing. You are capable of doing hard things. You are bigger than your fears. Take the first step today.

COMMUNITY STORY
Never stop believing

In 2011, I first came to Melbourne, Australia, under a spouse visa. I decided to enrol myself to become a certified chef, as back in my country, I worked mostly in the kitchen. To cut the story short, my son was diagnosed with autism while I was studying, and I got pregnant at the same time as I was offered a traineeship. The traineeship offer was withdrawn because I was pregnant, and I lost all interest. I gave birth and my daughter was also diagnosed with autism. At that point, I almost gave up. I had depression, anxiety, you name it.

It took me a while to move forward again, and then one day, one of my kids' NDIS coordinators asked me if I would like to be a support worker as he was surprised with my kids' progress and thought that I would be a good one. I accepted the offer and got the job. For the next six months, I worked to build my own business.

Currently, I have one employee and eight clients, and my business is earning good money. We recently bought land to finally start building a home. Now me and my husband have been focusing on watching our spending to pay off the land quicker.

Lesson learned: never stop, regardless of the trials you encounter along the way. You may detour on the way to your destination, but don't stop. Never stop dreaming.

Rocenie

FOCUS ON WHAT YOU CAN CONTROL

THINGS WE **CAN** CONTROL	THINGS WE **CAN'T** CONTROL
What we choose to believe	Past experiences (both yours and others' around you)
What we choose to feel	Other people's opinions and mindset
How we choose to think	Unexpected events
Our own actions and decisions	Other people's behaviours and reactions
How we take action	How the world changes around us

A key step towards a more stress-free and happier life begins with a mindset shift around what is in our sphere of control. It's not just about letting go of the things we can't control. It's about the understanding of and belief in the things we can control, and how this can have a drastic influence on our lives. Worrying and overthinking about the things we can't control, such as the past or other people's opinions, drains our energy and holds us back from focusing on what we can work on and change in our sphere of control. Here are some ways to focus less on what you can't control, and redirect that energy to the things you can control.

ACCEPT UNCERTAINTY

Life is uncertain. We never know what a day will throw at us, and there will always be unexpected and unplanned surprises and roadblocks along the way. What we do know about life is that every feeling, moment and situation is temporary. When life is good, savour the moment. When life is not so good, remember that this too shall pass, and you are brave and strong enough to overcome it. Accepting this reality, from both the good and bad perspective, will help you feel more at ease.

AVOID MAKING ASSUMPTIONS

If you find yourself making assumptions about a situation or guessing what someone may be thinking or doing — stop. Dwelling on our thoughts for extended periods of time can lead us to believe the assumptions we have created in our heads. Give yourself a reality check and focus only on the objective facts or truth.

BE ACCOUNTABLE ONLY TO YOURSELF

You will never be able to control other people's thoughts, opinions, behaviours or reactions. This is true in all areas of your life — at work, in your relationships and in your friendships. The only person you can control is you: what you choose to believe, what you choose to feel, how you choose to think and how you choose to act.

When you focus on your own choices and circumstances, you take back control of your life. Learn how to protect your energy, set and enforce boundaries, and improve your self-talk. Go after what you want. Advocate for the things that matter to you. Prioritise working on yourself and your goals.

LIVE IN THE MOMENT

When we focus on things that we can't control, we are trapped living in a future that does not yet exist. Bringing your mind back to the current moment you are living in can help you avoid overthinking and catastrophising about false realities. Mindset routines such as meditation or journaling are quick and effective methods of bringing your thoughts back into the moment.

MAKE FASTER DECISIONS

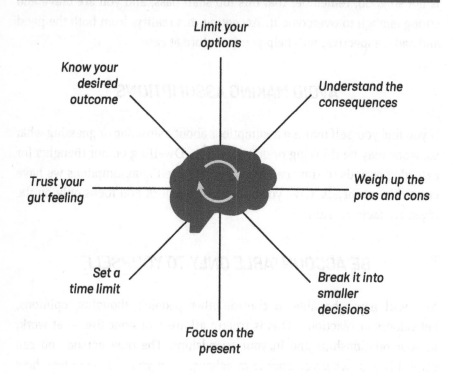

Limit your options

Know your desired outcome

Understand the consequences

Trust your gut feeling

Weigh up the pros and cons

Set a time limit

Break it into smaller decisions

Focus on the present

Every day, we make thousands of decisions.

What should I wear?

Where should I park my car?

What should I cook for dinner?

Should I send that risky text to my crush?

Should I accept this job offer?

Some of these are relatively straightforward. Others are more complex and serious. Learning how to make faster decisions is an important skill both in the workplace and in your personal life. Developing the ability to make good decisions quickly will help you avoid overthinking, feel more confident and become more productive.

KNOW YOUR DESIRED OUTCOME

To make a quick decision, you need to know up front what your desired outcome is. While you may be faced with multiple options, having a clear understanding of what your ultimate goal is will help streamline the decision-making process. If you are struggling to find a specific outcome, try closing your eyes and visualising yourself after you have achieved your goal. What are you feeling? How did you get there? Without knowing your desired outcome, your mind can't make a clear connection with the decision you are trying to make and how it connects to the ultimate goal. Try to be as specific as you can be from the start.

LIMIT YOUR OPTIONS

There may be endless options and different decisions that could be made in your scenario. Limiting your options to two or three helps you think clearer and minimises any delay to the decision-making process.

UNDERSTAND THE CONSEQUENCES

Understand and be comfortable with the consequences of the options you have as well as the consequences of not making a decision. Trying to make a decision without knowing this will set off your mind's natural fear mechanism and hold you back from making a quick decision.

WEIGH UP THE PROS AND CONS

All decisions have pros and cons. Grab a sheet of paper and write out a list of pros and cons side by side for every option. Be careful to not focus too much on only the pros or only the cons as this will misguide your decision making.

BREAK IT INTO SMALLER DECISIONS

If a decision seems too big and overwhelming, try breaking it down into smaller pieces. The overall goal will stay the same, but the smaller decisions required to get to this point can be made in increments.

FOCUS ON THE PRESENT

Making a decision should not involve over-analysing or hypothesising about unrealistic future outcomes that may or may not happen. Focus on the present and make the decision with the known information you have. While you need to understand how the decision impacts the future, this should not be the sole factor guiding you when choosing the best option.

SET A TIME LIMIT

Set a time limit for when the decision needs to be made. We often overthink decisions, which leads to increased stress and worry. Setting a time limit helps you to mitigate this anxiety and focus on finding a solution. A big life-changing decision may take a few weeks to resolve, but decisions in your daily life should be able to be made quickly.

TRUST YOUR GUT FEELING

It seems silly, but the old saying of 'trust your gut' has merit. Listening to your body's instinctive reaction can often help guide you toward the right decision. But be careful: sometimes our body's reaction can simply be a manifestation of our fear or anxiety when we are faced with something new that is outside our comfort zone. In this case, refer back to page 213 and channel your nerves into excitement at the opportunity for growth.

HOW TO STOP OVERTHINKING

- *Notice when you're overthinking*
- *Focus on problem solving*
- *Challenge your thoughts*
- *Write it out*
- *Distract yourself*

If you're a serial over-thinker, you're not alone. We've all scrutinised and mulled over a situation at least once in our lives: replaying awkward or failed scenarios in our head, re-typing an email 10 times so we don't come across as rude or second-guessing our abilities. The problem with overthinking is that the thoughts that are consistently on our minds become the reality that we experience. The thoughts that we can't get out of our head, and the emotions that these thoughts create, manifest into the action we end up taking (or not taking).

We overthink the issues in our lives and the decisions that need to be made by looking beyond the reality of the situation. This happens when we:

- begin to try and predict the future or over-evaluate the past
- hypothesise about the perceptions others may have about us or the situation we are in
- have too many options presented to us
- are experiencing ongoing or situation-based stress and anxiety.

A great quote that has always stuck with me is: 'If you stress too much about something before it happens, you basically put yourself through it twice'. Pretty powerful, hey? To help you tackle that voice in your head, the following pages include various strategies you can try to stop overthinking.

NOTICE WHEN YOU'RE OVERTHINKING

If you can't get an issue or a decision you need to make out of your head, take a minute to recognise that you are overthinking. Consider how long you have been thinking about this situation and whether it is starting to negatively impact your daily life. Are you unable to concentrate at work? Is it keeping you up at night? Are you disengaged from conversations with your partner or friends? Actively noticing when you are overthinking is a powerful first step.

CHALLENGE YOUR THOUGHTS

Next, it's time to fight back against your thoughts. For every worried or negative thought you have, challenge it with an opposing 'what if' statement.

What if things work out?

What if all my hard work pays off?

What if nothing bad happens?

What if I have a fun time?

What if I succeed?

Look at the situation you are in and have a serious debate with yourself as if you are discussing two sides of a situation or the pros and cons of a decision. This helps in understanding other perspectives you may not be able to see. Remind yourself of what you value and what is important to you in the situation.

WRITE IT OUT

A great way to combat overthinking is to write. Write out all the facts, background information and context to the situation. Write down all your thoughts and feelings. Write out the challenging 'what if' statements from page 232. Write out what is in your control. Write down the options you have available and the pros and cons of each option. It doesn't need to be neat or coherent, but getting all your thoughts out on paper can help you see the situation more clearly instead of jumping back and forth internally.

As you write, you may start to notice patterns in your overthinking. Are there certain areas of your life where it tends to happen more often, like at work? Do you tend to overthink certain activities or specific situations over and over again? Recognising the patterns will give you greater clarity of the root cause of the issue for you to solve.

FOCUS ON PROBLEM SOLVING

Instead of going over the same situation in your head over and over, refocus your energy on solving the problem. In some cases, the answer to the problem will be straightforward and, deep down, you know the right decision to make. Other times, it will be more difficult. In these circumstances, start by looking over all your notes from the previous point and see whether a clear solution stands out. Acknowledge that the solution may feel scary, but you shouldn't let the fear of the unknown or unfamiliar stop you from taking the next step. Alternatively, ask yourself 'What advice would I give someone else in the same position?' It's so simple, but sometimes removing yourself from the situation can give you the clarity you need.

DISTRACT YOURSELF

If your overthinking is getting the better of you, stop what you are doing and try to distract yourself. Go for a run, blast your favourite playlist and dance around the house, read a book or catch up with a friend. Whatever it is, getting your mind off things can really help.

HOW TO MOTIVATE YOURSELF

- Mix things up
- Pump some music
- Declutter your space
- Take a break
- Adjust your goal size
- Remind yourself of your 'why'
- Try a new time-management strategy
- Find a mentor/role model
- Focus on one thing at a time
- Practise gratitude

Motivating yourself is not an easy task. You know when you write a big to-do list, but then you feel overwhelmed and end up procrastinating all day? Or when you say to yourself that you're going to wake up early to go to the gym before work, but can't seem to get yourself out of bed? Or when you set some big goals you want to achieve, but then you feel guilty because you haven't made any progress towards them? It can feel like a never-ending cycle, leaving you feeling frustrated and disappointed in yourself.

No-one feels motivated 100 per cent of the time. Motivation usually comes in waves, but there are several strategies you can implement to boost your self-motivation. And the biggest, yet the simplest tip of all? Just start. It seems so blatantly obvious, but most of the time the hardest step is the first one.

MIX THINGS UP

When our daily routine becomes stagnant, we are often left feeling uninspired and unmotivated. Mix things up and try adding something new to your routine, whether that be testing out a new class at the gym, organising a mid-week catch-up with your friends or starting a new hobby that you have been wanting to try for ages.

PUMP SOME MUSIC

One of the simplest things you can do when you are low in energy or motivation is to play your favourite music. Pick something that is upbeat or inspires you. Have a dance break or play it through your headphones as you work.

DECLUTTER YOUR SPACE

Take a few minutes to clean up your space, wipe down surfaces and put items back in their usual spot. Having an uncluttered home and workspace helps you think more clearly, feel more focused and prepare to tackle the next task.

TAKE A BREAK

Juggling work, your social life, family commitments, staying healthy and everything else in between can leave you feeling exhausted. It's important to take regular breaks to rest and re-energise. Stepping away from your never-ending tasks and to-do list will reinvigorate your motivation so you can be your best, both at work and in your personal life.

ADJUST YOUR GOAL SIZE

If a big goal in your life feels overwhelming, try breaking it down into a series of smaller goals so they feel more achievable. Smashing smaller goals increases your overall motivation as you can see tangible progress over shorter periods of time. I talk a bit more about this in chapter 12.

REMIND YOURSELF OF YOUR 'WHY'

What you are trying to achieve and the actions that you are taking to get there must come back to a purpose. There needs to be a motivation deeper than the surface level goals of getting a promotion, buying a new material object or improving your health. Ask yourself: 'Why am I working towards this? Why does this mean so much to me? How will I feel when I achieve it?' Dig deep and understand the true reason why you are working towards something. Continuously remind yourself of this whenever you are lacking motivation.

TRY A NEW TIME-MANAGEMENT STRATEGY

Deep dive into the next chapter of this book and implement some new productivity and time-management strategies. Whether it is time-blocking, the Pomodoro Technique or the Eisenhower Matrix, finding what works for you will keep you motivated.

FIND A MENTOR/ROLE MODEL

Learn from the success of others and the experiences they have been through to seek inspiration and motivation for your own life. This may be a trusted friend, a manager at work or someone else you admire. Ask them for advice, review how they achieved their success and take any lessons from their challenges and failures.

FOCUS ON ONE THING AT A TIME

Trying to simultaneously achieve 100 goals often results in little progress being made as you are spread too thin across them all. This lack of progress can leave you feeling deflated and ready to throw in the towel. Instead, prioritise one goal at a time that you can devote more time and energy toward.

PRACTISE GRATITUDE

If you feel frustrated and unmotivated with your progress, take some time out to practise gratitude. Reflect on how far you have come, and be grateful for the journey you are on. Never compare your position with others and acknowledge that you are on your own path. Practising gratitude and focusing on the positives in your life will allow you to self-motivate through many situations.

WHAT TO DO IF YOU FEEL LIKE GIVING UP

Acknowledge
that this is
hard

Remember
how far you
have come

Take a break

Remind
yourself of why
it's important
to you

Ask for help

Whether you are studying for final exams, training for a half marathon or completing a challenging project at work, sometimes you hit a point where you are ready to throw in the towel. Usually when this happens, we get so frustrated and overwhelmed that the idea of giving up completely is the only feasible option.

When faced with this situation, take a moment to step back and breathe. Acknowledge that what you are doing is hard and you have hit a roadblock. Remind yourself of why this is important to you and how you will feel once you accomplish it. If possible, give yourself a break. Take the night off, think about how far you have already come and spend some time relaxing or doing something you enjoy. Having a good night's rest and coming back fresh is often the best remedy.

Don't underestimate the power of asking for help. It's not a sign of weakness to tell your friend, colleague, boss or loved one that you are struggling and need some assistance. You are not a burden, and in most situations, people are very happy to support you in any way they can.

13
Productivity

PLANNING YOUR WEEK

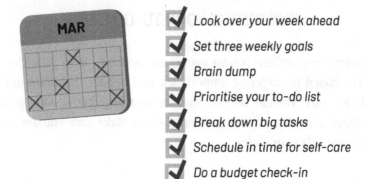

- ✓ Look over your week ahead
- ✓ Set three weekly goals
- ✓ Brain dump
- ✓ Prioritise your to-do list
- ✓ Break down big tasks
- ✓ Schedule in time for self-care
- ✓ Do a budget check-in

Planning your week in advance will allow you to hit the ground running and complete everything you set out to achieve. Set aside some time on Sunday evening to work through the following list and set yourself up for a successful week ahead!

LOOK OVER YOUR WEEK AHEAD

Start off by reviewing your calendar and schedule. Take note of any important deadlines, meetings, appointments and tasks you need to complete, both at work and in your personal life. This will form the basis of the rest of your planning.

SET THREE WEEKLY GOALS

Setting weekly goals is a great way to set short-term challenges for yourself and boost your motivation throughout the week. The best way to set weekly goals is to look at your larger monthly or yearly goals and work towards achieving a smaller chunk of this bigger goal by the end of the week.

BRAIN DUMP

Next up is to spend five minutes brain dumping everything that you need to get done in the week ahead on a sheet of paper. This could be anything from finishing off a client report, to sending an email to Sarah or booking a dentist appointment. Getting it onto paper means you can add it to your to-do list and schedule it into your calendar.

PRIORITISE YOUR TO-DO LIST

With everything written out on paper, the next step is to prioritise your to-do list based on urgency, importance and impact. By planning your week in advance, you can set priorities for the things you need to get done. Align these priorities to your greater goals to make sure you are staying on track towards your vision.

BREAK DOWN BIG TASKS

Make your weekly plan actionable by breaking down big projects and tasks into smaller pieces. Schedule each smaller piece into your calendar so you know exactly what you need to do each day.

SCHEDULE IN TIME FOR SELF-CARE

Always make time in your schedule for self-care and other activities that make you happy. Treat these like any other non-negotiable appointment and commit to them each week. Resting and re-energising is crucial to avoid burnout and stay healthy.

DO A BUDGET CHECK-IN

Don't forget to check in with your budget and see if you are on track for the month. Compare your actual spending against your budget and cut back on any areas where you may have over-spent.

REMINDERS FOR WHEN YOU FEEL OVERWHELMED

You are strong. There is nothing that you cannot handle.

Everything has always worked out in the past and it will this time too.

Be kind to yourself. You are doing an amazing job.

It's okay to say no or ask for help.

One day at a time, one task at a time, one step at a time.

If you're reading this right now, take a deep breath. Inhale through your nose and slowly exhale through your mouth. Repeat this another two times. Drop your shoulders. Unclench your jaw. Stand up and stretch your neck and body. Get some fresh air and go for a walk. When we are feeling overwhelmed, we tend to physically hold onto that stress in subtle ways. Take a moment to pause and relax your body's built-up tensions.

Grab a notebook and create a list of reminders for when you feel overwhelmed. The reminders here will get you started, but you can tweak them or add your own. Keep this list by your bed to read when you wake up every morning or on your desk to look at throughout the day.

Remember, you will get through this. You will get everything done. You've got this.

UNPRODUCTIVE WORK HABITS

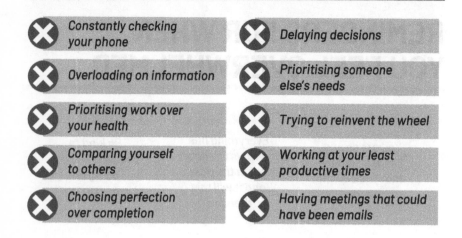

✖ Constantly checking your phone	✖ Delaying decisions
✖ Overloading on information	✖ Prioritising someone else's needs
✖ Prioritising work over your health	✖ Trying to reinvent the wheel
✖ Comparing yourself to others	✖ Working at your least productive times
✖ Choosing perfection over completion	✖ Having meetings that could have been emails

If you are feeling like you are constantly busy at work but reaching the end of the day with not much to show for it, you may be filling your time with unproductive work habits. A busy day does not mean an effective day at work. A productive day is finding the most efficient and effective way to achieve your desired outcomes. It is time to recognise and remove these unproductive work habits to take back control of your day.

CONSTANTLY CHECKING YOUR PHONE

Nothing exciting is happening on Instagram at 10:30 am on a Tuesday morning. Constantly checking your phone throughout the day will impact your productivity and reduce your motivation. Instead, have uninterrupted work periods and take regular breaks to grab a drink of water and check your phone, if required.

OVERLOADING ON INFORMATION

Information overload can cause you to feel overwhelmed and conflicted, and can stop you from getting on with work. Instead, focus on gathering only the information that is critical to making the decision. Learning how to synthesise large amounts of information is a skill, but it is a worthwhile one to develop.

PRIORITISING WORK OVER YOUR HEALTH

Your health must always remain your number one priority and all good employers will support this position. Being overloaded at work or stressed about an issue can lead to mental and physical health problems. Prioritise your health by speaking up to your employer/manager if you need support, taking time to adequately rest and setting clear boundaries to encourage your work-life balance.

COMPARING YOURSELF TO OTHERS

Comparing yourself to others in your workplace and what you see online is harmful to your productivity and motivation. It is unfair to yourself and the work you are doing. Instead, use comparisons to celebrate and be motivated by other people's success and take learnings that you can apply to your own journey.

CHOOSING PERFECTION OVER COMPLETION

Be careful to not prioritise perfection over completion. This doesn't mean you shouldn't complete your work to a high standard, but striving for perfection and setting unrealistic expectations for yourself leads to stress and procrastination. When you worry about doing something perfectly, you become stuck and struggle to do anything at all. Instead, focus on completing the crucial elements of a task or project to keep moving forward.

DELAYING DECISIONS

Decision making is a continual and critical part of your daily work life. Getting caught up in decision making will delay completing that activity and hold up moving on to the next task ahead. Refer to chapter 12 where we looked at how to make faster decisions.

PRIORITISING SOMEONE ELSE'S NEEDS

Learning to respectfully say 'no' in the workplace is a tool that everyone needs to learn. Instead of saying 'No, I don't have time', reframe your answer as a request to re-examine your priorities. Politely explain what you are currently working on and how long it will take you to complete. If the request for additional work is coming from your boss, this strategy gives them the opportunity to re-prioritise your work. If it is a colleague, they can understand that you can't take on any of their work.

TRYING TO REINVENT THE WHEEL

Not all tasks require a 'never before seen' solution. Completing a task efficiently is about achieving the desired outcome in the desired period of time. Typically this is done by utilising a tried-and-true method that you are comfortable will achieve your goal.

WORKING AT YOUR LEAST PRODUCTIVE TIMES

Don't fight against your body's natural energy timeline, work with it. If you are a morning person, plan your intensive work for first thing each morning and allocate less intensive work for the afternoons, and vice versa.

HAVING MEETINGS THAT COULD HAVE BEEN EMAILS

Before sending that meeting invite, ask yourself:

- What is the outcome I am trying to achieve?
- Does everyone have the information they need to make the decisions required and achieve the desired outcome?

If this is clear, there may not be any need for a meeting, and the same outcome could be reached with an email instead.

TURNING AROUND AN UNPRODUCTIVE DAY

- Prioritise
- Change your scenery
- Turn off notifications
- Take regular breaks
- Avoid multitasking
- Check in with an accountability buddy

In an ideal world, we would be productive 100 per cent of the time when we are at work. In reality, productivity ebbs and flows, and some days you may feel unmotivated, overwhelmed or simply not in the mood. The good news is that you can turn around an unproductive day by trying the following strategies to re-energise your mind and body to get more done.

PRIORITISE

Grab a sheet of paper and list your top three priorities that need to be accomplished by the end of the day. Setting priorities allows you to actively understand the critical tasks that you need to complete and how they are driving you forward towards your desired outcomes. If you are struggling to prioritise, try using the Eisenhower Matrix technique on page 246. Once you have set your three priorities, focus solely on getting these done by the end of the day and do not distract yourself with other tasks.

CHANGE YOUR SCENERY

Changing your scenery is a simple, yet effective way to reinvigorate your productivity. The next time you hit a slump in your day, change up your working space and head to your local café or a library. If that's not possible, can you move to a different room or space in the office or your house? You don't have to go very far, but the fresh outlook will refresh your mind and allow it to focus better on the task at hand.

TURN OFF NOTIFICATIONS

How often do you check your phone? With the constant flurry of calls, texts and social media, it's no wonder we are constantly distracted every time we hear the ringer or feel the vibration go off with a new notification. Switch your phone to do-not-disturb mode so you aren't tempted to check it every time a notification pops up. Alternatively, keep your phone off your desk where it's easy to reach and leave it in your bag or in another room.

TAKE REGULAR BREAKS

It's important to take regular breaks to refresh your mind. Utilise the Pomodoro Technique (see page 249) and work in uninterrupted 25-minute blocks followed by a five-minute break. Short bursts of focused work followed by a quick break helps you decompress, manage stress and stay productive for longer.

AVOID MULTITASKING

Trying to juggle five tasks at a time will only leave you feeling stressed out and frazzled. When your brain is trying to manage multiple tasks at once, and is constantly switching between them all, your attention is divided and interrupted. This is incredibly inefficient and can lead to more mistakes and heightened anxiety. Instead, focus on one task at a time and don't move on until it's done.

CHECK IN WITH AN ACCOUNTABILITY BUDDY

Having an accountability buddy helps you stay on track and be productive for longer. Tell a colleague or friend what your top three priorities are for the day or week and update them when you complete each one. Sharing your goals with an external party and having them keep you accountable is a highly effective method to increase your motivation and get more done.

MAKE AN END-OF-WEEK CHECKLIST

☑ *Finish off any quick tasks*

☑ *Update your to-do list*

☑ *Tidy up your workspace*

☑ *Reflect on your wins and challenges*

☑ *Switch off and enjoy your days off!*

An end-of-week checklist allows you to wrap up your work week with the satisfaction of knowing what you accomplished and the comfort of knowing what you have planned for the following week. Calling a physical and mental end to your work week signals to your brain that you can put aside any work-related activities or thoughts until you start again the following week. Your weekly check-in can be scheduled for any day that signifies the end of your week, not just a Sunday night. If you work across the weekend or at varying times throughout the week, try to select a day that fits best as a final day of your work week.

FINISH OFF ANY QUICK TASKS

Before wrapping up your work week, finish off any quick or last-minute tasks. That annoying piece of admin you know will only take five minutes? Clearing out your inbox from the last few days? Whatever it may be, if it'll take you less than 10 minutes, get it done.

UPDATE YOUR TO-DO LIST

Update your to-do list by removing completed tasks and adding any new tasks to be done the next week. Identify your top priorities and schedule them into your calendar, so when the new week starts, you can hit the ground running instead of spending an hour of your morning organising your day.

TIDY UP YOUR WORKSPACE

There's nothing better than starting a new work week with a clean workspace. Before you finish up for the week, pack away any papers and random items on your desk. Wash up any cups or mugs and use a disinfectant wipe to clean your computer screen, keyboard and mouse. You may be surprised how dirty they can get.

REFLECT ON YOUR WINS AND CHALLENGES

At the end of each week, reflect on your wins and accomplishments. Use this time to review any challenges or failures that you encountered, and identify the learnings and areas to improve for the week ahead. Reflect on the weekly plan and whether you achieved everything you had set for yourself. If not, reflect on why and then transfer these activities into the next weekly plan, where applicable.

SWITCH OFF AND ENJOY YOUR DAYS OFF!

As soon as you leave work at the end of your week, switch off. Remove notifications or delete the email app from your phone. That work email can wait a couple of days. Rest, spend time with loved ones, clean your home and work on your goals. Take time to relax and decompress so you feel re-energised when the new week comes around.

PRODUCTIVITY TECHNIQUES TO TRY

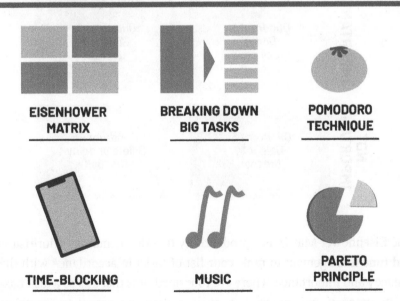

EISENHOWER MATRIX

BREAKING DOWN BIG TASKS

POMODORO TECHNIQUE

TIME-BLOCKING

MUSIC

PARETO PRINCIPLE

As we juggle the reality of work and life in the modern world, it often feels like the days where we feel super motivated and are working at our maximum capacity are few and far between. Our brains are constantly bombarded with new information, never-ending to-dos, urgent tasks and unexpected surprises. It is no surprise that the majority of us struggle with staying focused and being productive.

Learning how to increase your productivity will allow you to take control of your time and the way you spend it. By being in control, you will be able to progress towards your work and personal goals without feeling overwhelmed, while simultaneously maximising the time you have for the things that matter most to you. On the following pages, we will explore some of the most popular productivity techniques, as well as the SWS community's favourites. Test them out and find which ones work best for you.

EISENHOWER MATRIX

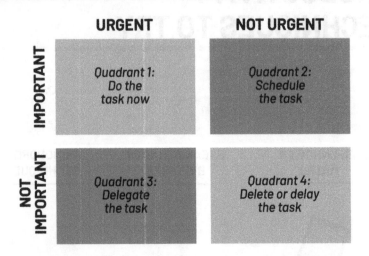

The Eisenhower Matrix is a productivity tool that combines prioritisation and time management to rank your list of tasks in accordance with their urgency and importance. There are four quadrants that assess a task based on its urgency and importance, scaling from not urgent to urgent and important to not important. The purpose of the matrix is to help you define whether a task should be completed now, planned to be completed later, delegated or delayed.

QUADRANT 1: DO THE TASK NOW

Any task you allocate to this quadrant requires your immediate action. These items typically include tasks that have fixed and fast-approaching deadlines that must be met to avoid any negative consequences. Some examples may include an urgent client report, a report due to your boss in the morning or needing to meet a submission deadline.

QUADRANT 2: SCHEDULE THE TASK

The tasks that you allocate to quadrant 2 are important, but usually do not have set deadlines or do not require immediate attention. In this case, schedule and plan for these tasks to be completed in the near future. Some examples may include networking and professional development. They will require forward planning and attention.

QUADRANT 3: DELEGATE THE TASK

The tasks in this quadrant do not require your specific skill set or expertise, and should be delegated. These tasks should not get in the way of your quadrant 1 tasks. Some examples may include administrative work, taking orders or formatting a presentation for a client. If you are unable to delegate the task, schedule it for a future time where it does not conflict with any tasks in quadrant 1 or 2.

QUADRANT 4: DELETE OR DELAY THE TASK

If a task is not urgent and not important, consider if you even need to complete it at all. If the task can't be deleted, delay it until you do not have other priority tasks on your list.

BREAKING DOWN BIG TASKS

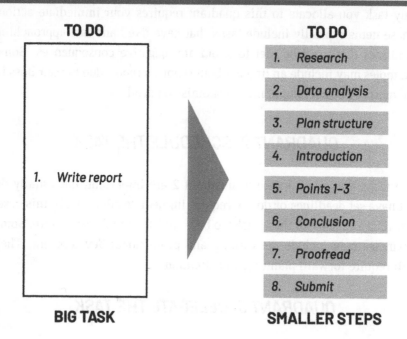

TO DO

TO DO

1. Research
2. Data analysis
3. Plan structure
4. Introduction
5. Points 1–3
6. Conclusion
7. Proofread
8. Submit

1. Write report

BIG TASK

SMALLER STEPS

When we are faced with a big task or project, our natural reaction is to feel overwhelmed with the work ahead and procrastinate about completing it. To avoid this, break the task or project down into smaller components and focus on completing one sub-task at a time. Create a logical order to complete each task so your mind has a clear way forward. For example, if you have a report that you need to write, break this down into research, data analysis, planning, writing the introduction, writing the main points and conclusion, then proofreading and submitting the final copy.

Doing so allows you to clearly see the steps you need to take to complete the big task and makes it feel a lot more manageable. To increase your productivity even further, allocate a deadline to complete each sub-task. This will keep you on track and accountable. Breaking down big tasks is best implemented alongside the Time-blocking technique and/or the Pomodoro Technique, which we will explore next.

POMODORO TECHNIQUE

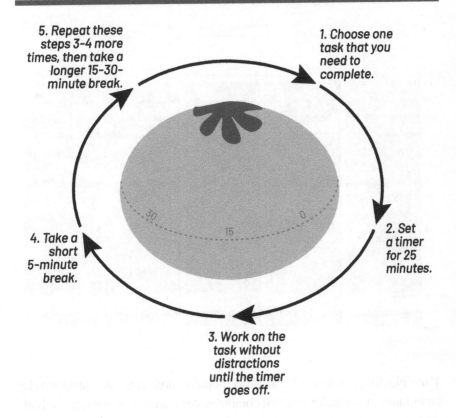

5. Repeat these steps 3–4 more times, then take a longer 15–30-minute break.

1. Choose one task that you need to complete.

2. Set a timer for 25 minutes.

3. Work on the task without distractions until the timer goes off.

4. Take a short 5-minute break.

The Pomodoro Technique was developed by Francesco Cirillo and involves working in 25-minute stints of uninterrupted work followed by a short five-minute break. Each cycle is called a 'pomodoro', which is the Italian word for tomato. After three to four pomodori, a longer 15- to 30-minute break is taken. The technique is widely popular as it utilises short, fixed timing and focused task allocation to increase productivity. Treat each pomodoro as a mini-deadline and challenge yourself to complete a task before the timer goes off. If you find yourself struggling to stay focused for the full 25 minutes or, conversely, you can work uninterrupted for longer, adapt the pomodoro cycle lengths to suit your needs and preferences.

TIME-BLOCKING

	Monday 6	Tuesday 7	Wednesday 8	Thursday 9	Friday 10
6 AM	Morning routine	Morning routine	Morning routine	Morning routine	Morning routine
7 AM	Exercise	Exercise	Exercise	Exercise	Exercise
8 AM	Get ready and commute	Get ready and commute	Get ready and commute	Get ready and commute	Get ready and commute
9 AM	Do Not Disturb	Client Meeting	Do Not Disturb	Do Not Disturb	Do Not Disturb
10 AM	Emails	Do Not Disturb	Emails	Emails	Emails
11 AM	Reporting	Emails	Break	Break	Break
			Client Meeting	Client Meeting	Client Meeting
12 PM	Lunch Break	Lunch Break	Lunch Break	Lunch Break	Lunch Break
1 PM	Team Meeting	Admin	Client Meeting	Do Not Disturb	Emails
2 PM	Break	Emails			Client Meeting
3 PM	Emails	Break	Break	Break	Break
4 PM		Client Meeting	Emails	Client Meeting	Reporting
5 PM	Planning	Planning	Planning	Planning	Planning
	Commute & Errands	Commute & Errands	Commute & Errands	Commute & Errands	Commute & Errands
6 PM					
7 PM	Dinner	Dinner	Dinner	Dinner	Dinner
8 PM	Self-care routine	Self-care routine	Self-care routine	Self-care routine	Self-care routine
9 PM	Reading	Reading	Reading	Reading	Reading
10 PM					

Time-blocking is one of the most popular and effective productivity techniques. It is a technique that combines short-term productivity methods with daily and weekly planning to help you get more done. Time-blocking involves planning your day in advance and allocating specific 'blocks' of time for each activity or commitment. As a best practice, your day should be split into 30-minute or 60-minute blocks of time and encompass your entire day — even beyond just work. Effective time-blocking will include your morning routine, exercise, self-care, personal admin, social activities, pre-sleeping routine and everything in between.

CHOOSE YOUR TIME-BLOCKING TOOL

Whether you prefer a digital or a physical planner, pick a tool that is suitable for your work and lifestyle. For digital options, you can use the calendar within your email platform (Google or Outlook) or your phone's in-built calendar app. These are the most straightforward options and include all the necessary features you require to effectively time-block. There are also a number of free and paid apps you can try out. If you prefer handwriting, you can use a physical diary planner or print out a copy of our Time-blocking template from **smartwomensociety.com/free-resources**.

DETERMINE YOUR WORK WEEK

For people with more flexible or changing work schedules, try and identify the times you will be working on a week-to-week basis. As your working hours will change, time-blocking becomes increasingly important. If you have set working hours, add these times into your time-blocking planning tool.

SET YOUR RECURRING TASKS

Each week you will have recurring tasks that you can predict and must be done. To effectively time-block, it is best to create a rigorous structure for these tasks so that you can properly plan and utilise the un-allocated time around them to maximum potential. Recurring tasks in your personal life may include your gym classes, grocery shopping, life administration or paying bills. In a work setting, your recurring tasks may include team meetings, reporting, invoicing or your commute.

BLOCK OUT 'DO NOT DISTURB' BLOCKS

Block out sections of time that are allocated to completing your most important tasks for that day. Call these your 'do not disturb' blocks. During this block, you will not be responding to emails, checking social media or replying to any 'quick questions'. This time is for focused, uninterrupted work to get your urgent and important tasks completed.

ALLOCATE TIME FOR NON-WORK ACTIVITIES

Staying productive relies on a balance of work and non-work activities. This will look different for everyone, but it is important to allocate key times in your week for non-work activities. Schedule this in before the week starts, and ensure your non-work activities are not swept to the side. Include any social events, exercise, self-care activities, your morning routine, watching your favourite TV show and anything else that makes you happy.

MUSIC

DEEP FOCUS WORK

*Instrumental only
(no lyrics)*

*Classical/
smooth jazz*

Electronic/Lo-fi

*White or
brown noise*

REPETITIVE TASKS

*Your all-time
favourite songs*

*Upbeat, pump-up
music*

Songs with lyrics

The sounds in your environment can have a significant impact on your productivity. Different sounds will either distract you from your work or act as the perfect background noise to keep you focused on the task ahead.

The use of music to stay focused is very subjective, but the styles of music listed here are widely accepted as resulting in increased productivity. To narrow down your selection process, think about the activity you will be doing. Is it an intensive task that requires your full concentration or a repetitive task that does not require much thinking?

We asked our community what their favourite music to listen to at work to be most productive is. Here are some of their responses:

'Brown noise has completely changed my life'—**Sabrina**

'Dark classical music'—**Trisha**

'Office or café background noise'—**Sarah**

'Lo-fi playlists are the best!' —**Hannah**

'Peaceful piano' —**Lilly**

'Some days when I have to get through heaps of repetitive admin work, I blast my favourite pump-up songs to keep me motivated and in good spirits' —**Jovana**

'Instrumental versions of my favourite musicals' —**Anna**

PARETO PRINCIPLE

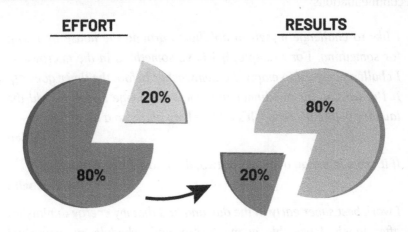

The Pareto Principle, or the '80/20 rule', relates to the generalised concept that 80 per cent of outcomes are derived from 20 per cent of causes. When looking at this principle through a productivity lens, it suggests that 80 per cent of your results come from 20 per cent of what you do, but the final 20 per cent of your results consume the remaining 80 per cent of your effort.

This can be a difficult idea to conceptualise as it does not sound intuitive at first. But think about your average work day. Does your most productive 20 per cent of the day result in 80 per cent of your work? Are 20 per cent of your clients responsible for 80 per cent of your business?

This thinking can assist with the prioritisation of tasks and activities that will provide the biggest impact with the lowest effort. Implement this principle into your daily life to focus on the top 20 per cent of your tasks that will result in 80 per cent of the outcomes you require.

YOUR FAVOURITE PRODUCTIVITY STRATEGIES

We asked the Smart Women Society community to share their favourite techniques to help them be productive. Here are some of their recommendations:

I like to challenge myself to do chores around the house as I wait for something. For example, if I have something in the microwave, I challenge myself to empty the dishwasher before the timer goes off. If I'm waiting for my dinner to cook, I challenge myself to fold the laundry before it's ready. It's a huge help and also a bit of fun.

—Ellen

If it takes less than a minute or two, do it now. Stop putting it off!

—Arabella

I work best super early in the day and find that my energy diminishes after lunch. I use this in my favour and schedule my important meetings and work early in the day, so I can do tasks that require less mental energy after lunch. Learning to work with my body's natural rhythms has been great for my productivity.

—Millie

Learn to say no more.

—Francesca

Think about the impact and intensity of each task. What impact or return will I get on the time and energy I spend on this task? How much brainpower does this task require? Doing this helps me prioritise my tasks and schedule them into my most productive hours.

—Liz

Shorten your deadlines or due dates. If it's due in a week, tell yourself it's due in 5 days and work towards that shorter deadline. This also gives you breathing room.

—Sanya

Try finding ways to systemise or streamline tasks you do regularly. I recently saved a heap of email templates for emails I send regularly and it saves so much time instead of having to write them from scratch each time.

—Whitney

Stop checking your emails every minute! It can wait. Do it twice a day max.

—Xenia

LOVE

In this section:

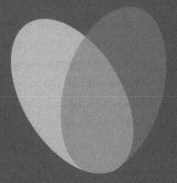

I once read a quote that said, 'People enter our lives for a reason, a season or a lifetime'. I didn't think about the quote too much at the time, but it had a nice memorable ring to it, so it stuck with me. As I've gotten older, I've realised that no-one comes into your life by accident. Every single person who crosses your path serves a purpose and can have a meaningful impact on you. Maybe they're there to teach you a lesson, build your confidence, recognise your potential or help you.

To my ex-boyfriend, who never made me feel good enough, I now know the importance of self-love and prioritising my relationship with myself first.

To my childhood best friend who moved halfway across the world to pursue her dreams, I am so proud of you even though we don't talk much anymore. You gave me the courage to pursue my own.

To my old coworkers who laughed behind my back about my 'little side hustle', thank you for giving me the motivation to grow my business and help hundreds of thousands of women all around the world.

I am so grateful for all these people. They taught me so much about myself and helped me grow exponentially as a person. Without them, I would not know what I stand for, to stop playing small and to stop caring so much about what others think.

Learn from the people who enter your life for a reason. These people may be in your life for a few minutes, days, months or sometimes even years. It's not about how much time someone spends with you, but how they affected your life in that time. Appreciate the people who enter your life for a season. These people are with you for a period in your life, be it at school, university, a certain job, a shared living situation or through another connection. Once your lives start diverging from that common place, person or interest, the relationship tends to fizzle. And lastly, nurture the people who enter your life for a lifetime. These people are simultaneously the rarest but most special people in your life. You may have weird distant phases, busy periods and ups and downs, but they will always be there for you no matter what.

You can never really predict what category someone will fall into. Sometimes the people you think will be in your life for a lifetime may end up being there only for a reason or a season. The only thing that's for certain is that the longest and most important relationship that you will ever have is with yourself. Don't wait for someone to give you the love you want and deserve. Learn to love every part of yourself, including your flaws, your imperfections and what makes you unique. Be your own biggest fan. Compliment yourself. Cheer yourself on. Focus on your growth. Work on healing your past trauma. Forgive yourself.

When you start prioritising yourself, magic happens. Not only will you look and feel better, but you will attract better. You won't settle for less. You won't lower your standards. You'll only accept people into your life who truly value your greatness and bring you nothing but happiness. Self-love is the best love.

14
Self-love

THINGS THAT DO NOT DEFINE YOU

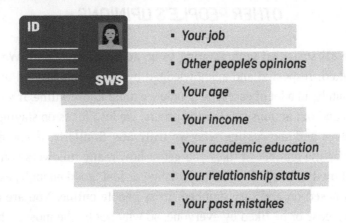

- Your job
- Other people's opinions
- Your age
- Your income
- Your academic education
- Your relationship status
- Your past mistakes

Growing up, we go through the journey of understanding who we are and how we see ourselves. It's a difficult pathway, filled with the opinions of others, the judgement of societal 'norms' and the pressures of our family and friends trying to define who we are. For many of us, it leads us to try to fit into a certain box so that we feel we belong, or achieve certain things so we feel important and worthy. We attach our self-worth to arbitrary things like our job title, our education or our income, while losing touch with what really matters and who we truly are. While there are a number of aspects of our lives that shape who we are, they definitely do not define us.

YOUR JOB

Society places a significance on the work and occupation of each individual, and often tries to group or stereotype people based on this. This filters down to an individual level, where many people still define themselves by their jobs and judge others using the same. How many times have you met someone new and the first thing they ask is: 'So what do you do?' We spend a lot of hours in our week at work. But at the end of the day, your job is just a job. It does not define your worth or who you are. It does not determine how intelligent or worthy or important you are. No matter what field you are in or where you work, you have value.

OTHER PEOPLE'S OPINIONS

We have all struggled with wanting to be accepted by others. We want to feel liked, respected and acknowledged by the people around us and, unfortunately, in a lot of cases, by people we don't know online. If we base our lives and our actions on pleasing others, we lose focus on staying true to ourselves and showcasing who we truly are. Similarly, if you define yourself by the number of likes you get or how many followers you have on social media, you will never be satisfied or feel 'good enough', as your worth is based on arbitrary numbers from people online. You are never going to please or be liked by everyone, so why not be the most authentic version of yourself.

YOUR AGE

Have you ever thought to yourself that you're 'too young' or 'too old' for something? Or maybe you've dreaded a birthday in the fear of getting older? We are conditioned to view our age as a defining factor of who we are and what we can or cannot do. We grow up being told that there is a particular timeline that our lives should follow, and that we should achieve certain things by certain ages or else we have 'missed the boat'. The truth is, there are no rules you have to follow. There are no age limitations on when you can do something. Stop constructing your whole life around your age and focus on living your life on your own terms.

YOUR INCOME

Your income or the amount of money you have does not define who you are. Society and social media portray a false narrative of defining our self-worth, success and happiness by the amount of money we earn or have. We all have different values and goals when it comes to money. We also all come from different backgrounds, with different circumstances, privileges and opportunities. Money provides a level of comfort, security and options. But it does not determine whether or not you are a good or happy person. What is important is that you foster a positive relationship with your money and use it to work towards your personal financial goals.

YOUR ACADEMIC EDUCATION

The pathways to a happy and successful life are endless, and they do not solely rely on a formal education, such as university or college. In many cases, the value you bring in your work life and career will be the result of your skills and experience, regardless of your formal education. You should not define yourself by your level of education, and nor should you look down on others who do not share the same level of education as you.

YOUR RELATIONSHIP STATUS

Whether you are single, in a relationship, separated or divorced does not define the person who you are. Having a partner does not mean that you are happier, more successful or have a better life. You can accomplish amazing things and be single. You can do the same and be in a relationship. Do not diminish or elevate your self-worth based on your relationship status. Take the opportunity to be the best version of yourself as an individual.

YOUR PAST MISTAKES

Your past mistakes and failures provide you with experiences and lessons you can take forward into your life. They don't define who we are or what we can go on to be. The weight of our past mistakes can hold us back from taking steps forward in our present life. While your past experiences, family life and the challenges and adversity you faced in your life shape your development, they do not define your current self.

For example, if you define yourself by a previous relationship and the mistakes you made, you are failing to acknowledge the effort you put in to heal and grow from the experience. Holding on to the past instead of looking forward towards future possibilities will hold you back from believing you are capable and going after new opportunities.

WHAT DOES DEFINE YOU

Here are some things that do define you:

- how you treat yourself, your partner, friends and family
- how you treat strangers
- your attitude
- your habits and routines
- your thoughts and actions
- your morals and values
- your kindness.

COMMUNITY STORY
Being authentically you

I have been a litigation lawyer in Montreal, Quebec, for almost 10 years. I have had confidence issues for as long as I can remember. I deliver the goods, but not without a lot of self-doubt. A few years ago I suffered from burnout, which, unfortunately, degenerated into severe depression. I wanted to be perfect in my role so badly that I made myself sick. You would never have thought I was depressed when I was at work. I laughed at all the jokes, I took initiative – in short, I committed myself even if it killed me a little more every day. To get through it, I had to refocus my boundaries at work, redefine my work methods and, most importantly, learn about myself.

Then one thing completely changed my life: I undertook gender transition to become the woman I have always been. This was not an easy path and involved a complete reorganisation of my life, including my professional life. I went from being a 'man' at work to being a woman. It's not the same approach, and it's a constant struggle to prove myself. I also needed to set boundaries, as it would have been easy for me to ignore the challenges I was facing. I not only learned to say 'no', but I learned to accept the consequences of saying no. Looking back, I realise that the consequences are quite positive.

I was afraid of how this transition would impact other people's perception of my skills, but it didn't. The support that I had from my employers was just perfect. So, I say to you, if you have this inner fear of being who you are: you have the right to be you and go for it. Maybe some people will judge you, but in the end, it doesn't matter. The important thing is to enjoy the time you are given in life. And you don't have to be going through a gender transition to apply this advice.

Émilie

HOW TO STOP FEELING GUILTY

Saying no and setting boundaries

Honest mistakes and failures

Taking a break

Celebrating your achievements

Asking for help

Changing your mind

Being unproductive and resting

Prioritising your goals and growth

Not replying to texts/calls immediately

THINGS TO STOP FEELING GUILTY ABOUT

Spending time alone

Putting yourself first

Guilt is a powerful emotion. Generally, it causes us to fixate on:

- what we did wrong
- what we should have said
- how we should have acted
- what we could have done differently.

While some guilt can be used to incite positive change in our lives, most of the time it lingers on our mind and can cause significant negative effects on our physical and mental wellbeing. Here are some tips to help you stop feeling guilty for things you don't need to.

ASSESS YOUR FEELINGS

Our minds have a way of using guilt as a cover for other deeper feelings, such as low self-esteem, resentment or anxiety. Instead of feeling confident in your decision to stay home on a Friday night to rest, you may feel anxious that your friends will think you're a selfish or bad person.

This anxiety results in feelings of guilt. The next time you feel guilty, think about the root cause making you feel this way, and question the validity and accuracy of these feelings.

ACCEPT YOUR PAST

We all make mistakes along the way, so there is no reason to hold on to these feelings. Take time to reflect on your past mistakes and experiences. Accept that these have occurred in the past and give yourself permission to let go of any guilt that you may still be holding on to. It's time to focus on the present moment and opportunities instead.

OWN YOUR DECISIONS

If you make a decision, it is your responsibility to own it. You are setting these boundaries, taking a break, saying 'no' or prioritising your goals for a reason. When you start feeling guilty about a decision you have made, remember why you made it in the first place. Take control of the decision, and be confident in the reasons behind it.

CHANGE YOUR PERSPECTIVE

We often overthink decisions or issues and struggle to see the bigger picture around us. Something small may seem larger than it is until you look at it from a new perspective. If you feel guilty about a mistake or changing plans on someone, take a step back and ask yourself if your guilt makes sense. It may also be helpful to ask yourself: 'What would I tell a friend in a similar scenario?'

DEVELOP EMPOWERING SELF-TALK

The thoughts you continually keep are the ones that will manifest into your life. The guilt of not replying to a text immediately or for taking a break or for asking for help is the result of you thinking: 'Am I being rude?'

or 'I'll never get this done' or 'I am not good enough'. When we reframe these limiting beliefs into empowering beliefs, we start to reprogram our minds into accepting the reasoning behind our actions and removing the guilt associated with them. Change these thoughts to: 'I'm prioritising my own wellbeing' or 'I will do my best to get this done' or 'I'm still learning and improving'.

DON'T QUESTION YOUR PRIORITIES

Feeling guilty often leads us to question and become flexible with our priorities. You have made your priorities clear for a reason. Keep these at the front of your mind when making decisions, and don't second guess or question their importance. You do not need to justify or rationalise what you choose to put first.

HOW TO STOP CARING ABOUT WHAT OTHER PEOPLE THINK

People worry more about their own lives and probably don't notice or think about most of the things you think they do.

Remind yourself that someone's negative comments are a reflection of their own insecurities.

Surround yourself with positivity. Remove or distance yourself from toxic people and situations.

You can't please everyone and that's okay.

Focus on being the best version of yourself. Work on your own self-love and acceptance.

If you always worry about what others think of you, or you allow their opinions — or what you perceive their opinions to be — to take control of your thoughts and actions, ask yourself this: How often do you think about other people? How often do you really care about how they live their lives or what they do? Probably not that often, right? The same applies to you. People are so consumed by their own lives and their own worries and issues that they probably don't notice or give a second thought to most of the things you think they do.

There will always be people in the world who have something negative to say. This could be directly to your face, via an online comment or message, or behind your back. Instead of allowing these negative comments to hold power over you and your self-worth, remember that these comments almost always stem from the person's own experience and their insecurities, jealousy and unhappiness. A happy, confident person does not have the time or desire to spread negativity about others.

What's more important is surrounding yourself with genuine people who will support you, keep you accountable and provide constructive criticism with the sole purpose of helping you grow and flourish. On a personal level, work on yourself and understand what truly makes you happy. Life is short. Be confident in the decisions you make, and live your life in accordance with your authentic values. You do not have to wait for someone else to see your value before you start believing in yourself. Do not shrink yourself, play small or water yourself down to please others.

The reality is you will never be able to please everyone. You could be the nicest, kindest and most selfless person in the world, and there will still be someone who has something negative to say about you. Once you accept the fact that you will never be able to control other people's thoughts and opinions, you can fully focus on becoming the best version of yourself.

HOW TO BOOST YOUR SELF-CONFIDENCE

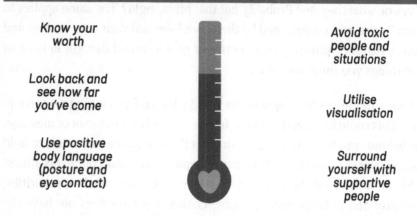

Know your worth

Look back and see how far you've come

Use positive body language (posture and eye contact)

Avoid toxic people and situations

Utilise visualisation

Surround yourself with supportive people

We are often our own biggest critic. We fill our heads with irrational thoughts, fears, self-doubt and excuses, which leaves us feeling stressed, anxious and holds us back from achieving our goals. The key to overcoming this is to build confidence in who you are and controlling your thoughts and actions.

KNOW YOUR WORTH

To be truly confident, you must know your worth and how much you bring to the table. Once we are able to believe in ourselves and accept our strengths and weaknesses, we develop the confidence to get through any life situation. Practise gratitude and engage in positive self-talk. Forgive yourself for past mistakes. Stop comparing yourself to others and embrace what makes you unique.

LOOK BACK ON HOW FAR YOU HAVE COME

Thinking about past successes or something you are proud of is a quick and effective tool to push you out of a low-confidence state. Re-live the moment when you achieved an accomplishment, remind yourself of the actions you took, how it felt during the process and how you achieved that outcome. Reminding yourself of how much you have achieved and of all the challenges you have overcome in the past helps to re-frame your mind to think in a more positive way.

USE POSITIVE BODY LANGUAGE

Your body language is a tell-tale sign of whether you are feeling confident or are in a state of low confidence. When we think about a confident person, we imagine them sitting up straight or standing up tall with their shoulders back, and walking with purposeful strides. This is for good reason. Projecting confident body language can help our minds believe that we are confident. An extension of this is in the clothes you wear. Dress up for you, not for others. Wearing an outfit you love and feel good in can dramatically increase your confidence.

AVOID TOXICITY

Take yourself out of any toxic environment or relationship that is putting you down and negatively impacting your self-confidence. If you have a friend who always has a negative comment to make about you, set up boundaries and distance yourself from interacting with them. Same goes for that one family member who constantly judges your career or life choices.

UTILISE VISUALISATION

Visualisation is a powerful technique that is used by self-confident people on their journey to success. It involves regularly thinking about achieving your goal and how you made it happen. This sends a message to your brain that achieving this goal has already happened, so when you are faced with the scenario in real life, your brain is already familiar with the situation and approaches it with certainty and confidence. For more on this, see the discussion on goal setting in chapter 12.

While confidence should come from within, the people we surround ourselves with play an important role in pushing us along in times of need. No matter what you are trying to achieve, surround yourself with people who give you confidence and positive support. This might be that one friend who understands your goals and is cheering you on along the way; joining a group of similar-minded people who support each other; or finding a mentor/coach who can be there to guide you and push you to become the best version of yourself.

HOW TO CELEBRATE YOURSELF

- Dress up in your favourite outfit

- Buy yourself fresh flowers

- Make a list of 10 things you like about yourself

- Take yourself out on a solo date

- Take a break and unwind

- Reflect on and be proud of everything you've accomplished in the last year

- Have a pamper night

The longest relationship you will ever have is with yourself. Why is it then that it is often the one relationship that we treat the most poorly? We talk a lot about cultivating our friendships and relationships, but nurturing the relationship we have with ourself is equally, if not more, important. Invest love, time and energy into becoming your own biggest fan and celebrating yourself along the way. The more you celebrate yourself, the more your happiness and confidence rises.

It's not bragging. It's not selfish. And you don't have to wait until your birthday. Celebrating yourself is simply about recognising and acknowledging how amazing and unstoppable you are. It's about making a commitment to prioritise yourself and focus on your needs. It's about celebrating every win, no matter how big or small. Because you deserve it.

There are many ways to celebrate yourself daily, weekly and yearly.

DAILY CELEBRATIONS

- Remind yourself of your favourite qualities.
- List five things you're proud of yourself for.
- Pick up your favourite sweet or a fresh bunch of flowers.
- Accept compliments by saying 'thank you' instead of deflecting them.
- Get dressed up in your favourite outfit.
- Do something that makes you happy.

WEEKLY CELEBRATIONS

- Schedule a pamper night.
- Reflect on the work/task you completed and your progress towards your goals.
- Take yourself out on a solo date.
- Take a day off just to 'do nothing'.

YEARLY CELEBRATIONS

- Make that purchase that you have been saving for all year (as long as it aligns with your financial goals and values).

- Book yourself a holiday or weekend away with your partner/ friends/family.

- Reflect on everything you have accomplished in the past year.

COMMUNITY STORY
Putting in the self-work

I've been on a self-love journey for the last few years: unlearning bad habits and thoughts and re-learning more positive patterns. I've learnt to set and maintain boundaries, to forgive myself for past mistakes, to come to terms with the fact that life is always changing (for better and for worse).

Transitioning from my old self to my new self has been difficult, scary and new. I had to come face-to-face with a lot of things I didn't like about myself. But I'm really proud of myself for doing the 'inner work'. I have a whole new perspective on my life, and approach everything with confidence and an open mind. It's taken a while to get to this point, but there's truly no better feeling.

Lana

THINGS YOU DON'T NEED TO JUSTIFY

What you like doing in your free time

Your relationship status

Your hobbies and interests

Cutting off toxic friendships and relationships

Your goals and priorities

Your emotions and feelings

Taking a new direction in your life/career

When we let the opinions of others dictate our actions and feelings, we get distracted from pursuing our own true happiness. Feeling like you need to justify your decisions and behaviours can stem from personal life experiences, how you have grown up, or it could be a product of your current environment. When someone questions a decision you have made or your viewpoint on a topic, they are often projecting their own values and insecurities onto you. Comments like, 'Why aren't you married yet?' or 'You're changing careers? What a waste of all those years!' or 'If I were you, I would never have done that' are examples of this.

We all see things differently in this world. We all have different values, goals and definitions of fulfillment and happiness. There is no 'right' path or timeline that we have to follow. The only thing that truly matters is that you live your life according to your own set of goals and priorities, and make the best decisions for you based on your own wants and needs. Never feel like you have to justify any of the actions, behaviours, feelings or values that are pushing you towards your own goals and growth.

TIMELINES DON'T EXIST

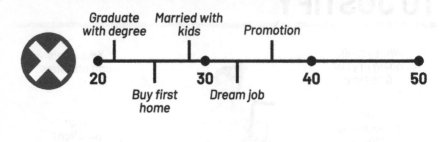

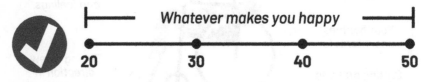

Life is not a race. Nor is it a competition. There is no designated time for anything in your life. There's no checklist of milestones to tick off. There are over seven billion people on this planet and every single person cannot follow the exact same arbitrary timeline. You're not 'behind' in life. There is no expectation to do anything by a certain age. You don't have to get a degree by 21, be married by 30 and land your dream role before you turn 35. It's all made up.

There's no one 'right' pathway to follow. You are on your own path and what route you take, where you are headed and when you will get there is totally unique to you. The only rule in life is to pursue what makes you happy. To find and fulfil your purpose. And to wake up every morning filled with gratitude for the life you have created for yourself.

THINGS YOU WILL NEVER REGRET

Complimenting
a stranger

Practising
random acts of
kindness

Advocating for
causes you
believe in

Speaking up
for yourself

Telling a
loved one
how much
they mean to
you

Helping
someone in
need

Putting in
effort

There are many things in life that we will never regret doing. On a personal level, you will never regret putting in effort, believing in yourself or upholding your values. No matter the outcome, the most important thing is knowing that you gave your all to your goals, work and relationships. This works hand in hand with always believing in yourself and having the self-confidence to live your life authentically. If you can stay true to yourself, you will be able to stand up for yourself and advocate for the causes you believe in.

On a broader level, you will never regret expressing your love and admiration for the important people in your life. There are not too many more satisfying acts in life than being able to help someone and bring a smile on their face. This can be as simple as giving someone a compliment, telling someone how much they mean to you, performing a random act of kindness or helping someone who you know is in need. Seeing a smile on someone's face will promote the positivity within you, and boost the mood of both you and the other person.

15

Setting boundaries

WHY BOUNDARIES ARE IMPORTANT

- *Allows you to feel respected by those around you*
- *Requires you to stop putting other people's feelings and needs before your own*
- *Boosts your self-esteem and confidence*
- *Creates a feeling of peace and safety*
- *Reduces feelings of confusion and anxiety*
- *Creates less conflict in relationships*
- *Ensures you prioritise your own needs and happiness*
- *Sets clear expectations for others*

Boundaries refer to the physical or emotional standards that we set for how we would like to interact with the people in our immediate environment.

They include standards and expectations for how we want to be treated by others and how we want others to act when they are around us. Some examples of people who you can set boundaries with include your partner, family members, friends, colleagues and your boss. Establishing boundaries not only helps to ensure that your emotional and physical needs are addressed, but they also foster an environment that is safe and respectful for all parties involved.

COMMON MYTHS ABOUT BOUNDARIES

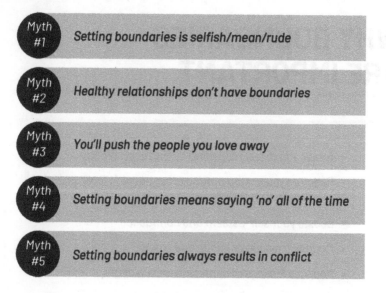

Myth #1 — Setting boundaries is selfish/mean/rude

Myth #2 — Healthy relationships don't have boundaries

Myth #3 — You'll push the people you love away

Myth #4 — Setting boundaries means saying 'no' all of the time

Myth #5 — Setting boundaries always results in conflict

Setting healthy boundaries can positively impact all our relationships, so what holds us back? There are many myths that surround setting boundaries that give it a negative and confrontational name. This is not at all true, as the core idea of setting healthy boundaries is to foster peace, positivity and respect in the relationships we have to ensure our needs are being met. These myths are the product of how people may have experienced unhealthy boundaries, which are filled with anger, resentment and selfishness. Remember, the only people who get upset when you set boundaries are the people who benefited from you having none in the first place.

MYTH 1: SETTING BOUNDARIES IS SELFISH/MEAN/RUDE

The purpose of setting boundaries is to understand and protect your own wants and needs, and to communicate those wants and needs to others in a way that is both clear and respectful. By doing so, you are able to establish the foundation of how you would like to be treated and ensure that all your relationships are able to develop in a way that is comfortable for all parties involved. Setting and enforcing boundaries should not be argumentative or aggressive. You are simply setting guidelines to protect your emotions, time and energy.

MYTH 2: HEALTHY RELATIONSHIPS DON'T HAVE BOUNDARIES

Healthy boundaries are essential for any kind of relationship. The idea that healthy relationships do not have boundaries is simply not true. In fact, the strongest relationships have clear boundaries that are enforced and respected by both parties. When we establish a boundary with someone, we are providing them with guidance that will allow them to build a stronger relationship with us rather than pushing them away.

MYTH 3: YOU'LL PUSH THE PEOPLE YOU LOVE AWAY

In relationships where you have not set any boundaries or have limited boundaries, the other person has the opportunity to take advantage of you. When you start to set and enforce new boundaries with them, you may experience some pushback. Do not let this deter you. Remember, you are establishing boundaries to improve your relationship and set clear expectations for how you would like to be treated. If the person is not respectful of your boundaries and repeatedly crosses them, then it may be time to rethink if you want to pursue the relationship any longer.

MYTH 4: SETTING BOUNDARIES MEANS SAYING 'NO' ALL OF THE TIME

Saying 'no' is, without a doubt, an essential part of setting up your boundaries. Saying 'no' is a simple and effective tool for taking control of your time, which then allows you the opportunity to focus on yourself and your needs. But setting boundaries is more than just saying 'no' all the time. It is about protecting your time, energy and emotions so you can ultimately say 'yes' to more of the things that matter to you.

MYTH 5: SETTING BOUNDARIES ALWAYS RESULTS IN CONFLICT

While it may take some adjusting for some people when you do set boundaries, conflict is never part of a healthy boundary process. Boundaries are grounded in respect and should result in strengthened relationships. If, at any stage, setting your boundaries results in conflict, aggression or arguments, it is time to reassess your relationship with that person and whether you wish to continue with it. Respect their process for understanding your boundary, but don't take a step back. You should never adjust your boundaries because others are not happy with them.

TYPES OF BOUNDARIES

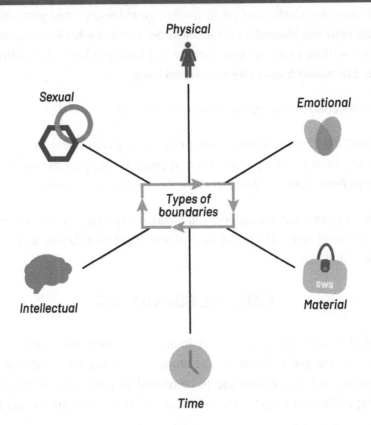

Physical

Sexual

Emotional

Types of boundaries

Intellectual

Material

Time

Setting boundaries can apply to all aspects of your life. They can be broken down into six categories: physical, emotional, material/financial, time, intellectual and sexual boundaries.

PHYSICAL BOUNDARIES

Physical boundaries refer to all your physical needs, such as resting, eating and drinking. They also cover your personal space and contact. Physical boundaries may sound like:

I can't right now, I need to rest.

I need some space.

I'm not a big hugger; I prefer handshakes instead.

EMOTIONAL BOUNDARIES

Emotional boundaries are set to protect your feelings and your energy. Setting emotional boundaries is about understanding what level of emotion you are willing to accept from people and how much you are willing to share. Emotional boundaries may sound like:

I'm not comfortable talking about this right now.

I don't like that whenever I open up about my feelings, you judge me and make comments that put me down. If you can't support me and respect my feelings, I am not going to share them with you anymore.

I am here to listen and support you through this difficult time. I have a lot of personal things I'm trying to deal with right now. Are we able to talk about this later?

MATERIAL BOUNDARIES

Material boundaries refer to your items and possessions, such as your home, car, computer, furniture and money. These boundaries define how you would like your belongings to be treated by others and what you are willing to share or keep to yourself. Material boundaries may sound like:

Can you please not eat in my car?

I'm happy to lend you my dress for the party, but I'll need it back by Monday.

I can't lend you any more money, but I am happy to help in another way.

TIME BOUNDARIES

We only have 24 hours in a day, and we need to spend them wisely. Time boundaries are set to protect your time so you can focus on your priorities. Time boundaries may sound like:

I can come, but I can only stay for an hour. I have a lot to do at home.

I can't make it this weekend, but I appreciate you asking.

I can help you with that. My hourly rate is …

INTELLECTUAL BOUNDARIES

Intellectual boundaries are set to protect your thoughts and ideas. They also include respect and understanding of other people's opinions and views. A key aspect of healthy intellectual boundaries is a willingness to engage in discussion without being belittled, shut down or dismissed. Intellectual boundaries may sound like:

I understand what you are saying, but I disagree.

This is my opinion, so I would appreciate if you did not belittle me.

I don't think we should continue this conversation right now.

SEXUAL BOUNDARIES

Sexual boundaries refer to the understanding of preferences, consent, agreement, respect and privacy with respect to any form of sexual interaction. Sexual boundaries may sound like:

I don't like that. Let's try something different.

I'm not comfortable right now for this to progress further.

Asking for consent.

HOW TO BUILD HEALTHY BOUNDARIES

- Know yourself
- Understand the relationship type
- Give and take
- Practise saying 'no'
- Remove any fear or guilt
- Take your time
- Start slow and keep it simple

People who prioritise themselves and are able to implement well-defined boundaries experience less stress and have greater self-belief and confidence. Setting boundaries might not come instinctively to you, and it can be scary doing it for the first time. Be patient with yourself and take small steps to practise standing up for yourself and your needs.

KNOW YOURSELF

Prior to establishing boundaries in any relationship, understand what your values and needs are. This will allow you to define the non-negotiables for what the boundary is trying to achieve.

Ask yourself:

- What is important to me in life?
- What do I want to stand for?
- What do I value doing with my time?

UNDERSTAND THE RELATIONSHIP TYPE

The boundaries that you set will vary among the different people in your life. For example, the boundaries you set with your partner will be very different from those that you set with colleagues at work. It is important to understand the type of relationship that you have with the person and the regular interactions you have with them. Boundaries can also be rigid or flexible depending on the circumstances and individual person. Rigid boundaries are non-negotiable guidelines that are never adjusted no matter what, whereas flexible boundaries may change over time and with different people.

GIVE AND TAKE

Any relationship you have should be reciprocal and involve an element of give and take from both parties. In most cases, this reciprocity should be equal, but in some cases (such as in parent-child or boss-employee relationships), it may be more heavily weighted to one side. What is important is knowing that the value, respect and time you have for a relationship is being reciprocated, and no-one is being taken advantage of.

Consider the relationships you have in your life and whether they are reciprocal. What do you give to this relationship? What do you get out of it? Is this unfairly weighted? If yes, why? Answering these questions honestly will help you better understand the appropriate boundaries that need to be set.

PRACTISE SAYING 'NO'

Being able to say 'no' is a powerful way to take back control. When you set boundaries, you are doing more than just saying 'no'. You are giving yourself back the time to say 'yes' to the priorities you want to focus on. It can be difficult to start saying 'no' to people who you have always agreed with and kept the peace with, but practise beforehand at home to help you build up your confidence for the real deal. Communicate your no's calmly, clearly and confidently. There is no requirement for you to justify or overexplain your reasoning.

REMOVE ANY FEAR OR GUILT

Do not allow people's opinions or reactions to make you feel afraid, ashamed or guilty for enforcing your boundaries. If you know setting your boundaries with a particular person may become confrontational, it is best to avoid using phrases such as 'you did' or 'you do'. This can come across as an accusation and they may feel defensive. Try using 'I' statements, such as, 'I feel (feeling) when you do (action) to me.' If the other person becomes confrontational when you are setting the boundary with them, avoid reacting emotionally. Leave the conversation after making your boundary clear and give them time to process and understand the change. Enforcing your boundaries is about protecting your own peace of mind and wellbeing. While others may think that your boundaries are impacting them, stay firm and don't let their opinion or perspective affect you.

TAKE YOUR TIME

Setting boundaries can be tricky. It is best to plan and implement your boundaries when you have a clear mind and are not being influenced by reactive emotions. Don't make important decisions when you are tired, stressed or emotional. Sleep on it and speak to the person calmly the next day to discuss your feelings and establish your boundary.

START SLOW AND KEEP IT SIMPLE

Having a difficult conversation with your partner, friend or family member is never easy, so start off slowly and build it up gradually. Avoid sitting down with someone and discussing every little issue you have with them, when, ultimately, there may only be one or two key boundaries that you need to set.

BOUNDARIES WITH FRIENDS

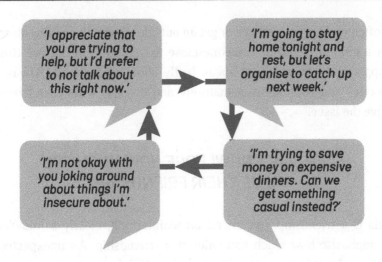

'I appreciate that you are trying to help, but I'd prefer to not talk about this right now.'

'I'm going to stay home tonight and rest, but let's organise to catch up next week.'

'I'm not okay with you joking around about things I'm insecure about.'

'I'm trying to save money on expensive dinners. Can we get something casual instead?'

Boundaries are an essential part of all healthy, strong friendships. It can be difficult, however, to set boundaries with our friends, especially if we have known them and accepted certain behaviours of theirs for many years. Reflect on the different friendships in your life, ranging from your closest friends to those who you may see every so often. Are there certain things these friends do that bother or upset you? If you answered 'yes' to this question without hesitation, that is a strong indicator that you need to set boundaries around it. Follow these steps to get started.

STEP 1: OPEN THE DIALOGUE

Setting boundaries with friends is best done calmly and with an open dialogue. This allows both of you to discuss the boundary and how you feel about it. Ask your friend to grab a coffee and, when the time is right, explain to your friend what has been on your mind and how you would like to address it by establishing a boundary. While it is tempting sometimes to just avoid the entire issue, letting it sit in the back of your mind will only cause it to grow larger and turn into something that may be irreparable. Most of the time you will find that your friend is not knowingly or intentionally trying to upset you, and having an honest conversation is the best way forward.

STEP 2: DON'T GOSSIP/SPEAK BADLY ABOUT YOUR FRIEND

It is often good to seek advice or get an outside perspective of the situation from a mutual friend or someone close to you. But do not use this as an opportunity to gossip or speak badly about your friend. Always be respectful and communicate maturely and directly with your friend to resolve the issue.

STEP 3: ACKNOWLEDGE HOW MUCH YOU VALUE THEIR FRIENDSHIP

If this is a friendship you intend on maintaining, clearly acknowledge and emphasise how much you value their friendship. An unexpected or significant boundary can sometimes feel hurtful, but reiterate that you are doing so to strengthen your friendship for many years to come.

STEP 4: USE 'I' STATEMENTS

When discussing a new boundary with your friend, focus solely on your own feelings and avoid directly attacking them. The conversation is to help them to understand your perspective and is not an attack on their own behaviour. Using phrases such as 'You never think before you talk' will divert the conversation to arguing about their behaviour and cause more issues. Instead, use 'I' phrases, such as 'I get uncomfortable when you make comments about my appearance'.

STEP 5: BE KIND BUT FIRM

No matter your communication style, you need to be sure that the other person understands that you are very serious about setting this boundary, and that you are not going to compromise on protecting your peace. Be kind but firm when stating your boundary.

COMMUNITY STORY
Navigating a toxic friendship

I met a girl on my first day of university and we instantly became best friends. We attended all our classes together, and went out and had lots of fun. Over time, I started noticing her behaviour and attitude changing. She would bring me down, telling me I'm not qualified enough to apply for a certain job, or that I shouldn't be too ambitious, so I don't get disappointed. Every time I tried to hang out with other friends, she would get jealous, asking who I'm texting, and complaining that I don't spend time with her anymore.

I didn't like the person she was turning into, but I felt guilty because we shared so many great memories. It was draining and I always left our interactions feeling really bad about myself. This wasn't how a 'best friend' was meant to treat you. I started researching how to navigate it all and learnt about boundary-setting. I started small, voicing when something she said or did crossed my boundaries.

She pushed back hard, and said I was being dramatic and unreasonable. It was hard to not back down, but I knew I had to stay calm and strong in enforcing my boundaries to protect my own mental health and peace of mind. Her behaviour didn't really change, and I stopped reaching out as much. Once I gave myself space and limited my interactions, it felt like a huge weight was off my shoulders. I literally felt like I could breathe again. We don't speak much (if at all) anymore, and I am proud of standing up for myself and not being pushed around.

Stephanie

HOW TO SET BOUNDARIES AT WORK

- *Taking your lunch break*
- *Communicating concerns about your workload*
- *Setting 'do not disturb' time blocks for focused work*
- *Saying 'no' to unreasonable overtime or requests*
- *Not checking work emails out of hours*

Boundaries at work can refer to both the boundaries you set with yourself and also the boundaries set with your colleagues or managers. Having clear work boundaries ensures that you feel comfortable in your workplace and helps to maintain a positive work-life balance.

SETTING WORK BOUNDARIES WITH YOURSELF

Setting boundaries for yourself at work will ensure you can maintain a healthy relationship with your job. Without these in place, you may find yourself experiencing workplace burnout, which can lead to decreased productivity, feeling frustrated and exhausted, prolonged negativity and low job satisfaction.

Your personal work boundaries may include:

- logging off from all forms of communication at the end of the workday
- turning off notifications after work hours to avoid seeing late-night emails
- defining a workload capacity with your manager to avoid being overstretched

- setting clear working hours and not accepting meetings outside of your normal work hours

- setting boundaries around work calls outside of hours

- scheduling a non-negotiable lunch break each day to take a break

- saying 'no' to additional work from a colleague without discussing it first with your manager

- using your sick leave when you are unwell without feeling guilty

- not doing any work when you are on annual leave.

SETTING WORK BOUNDARIES WITH YOUR COLLEAGUES/MANAGER

Setting boundaries with your colleagues is not only about the actual work you are doing, but also about any physical or social interactions. Setting work boundaries with your colleagues may look like:

- saying 'no' to additional work your colleague asks you to do (e.g. 'I am at capacity and can't assist with that work today.')

- saying 'no' to additional work from your manager (e.g. 'I am currently working on [insert tasks], but I am able to do this work if you would like me to prioritise it instead.')

- not needing to answer non-urgent questions or help with a task straight away (e.g. 'I am finishing up a task and will be able to assist once I am done.')

Setting social/physical boundaries with your colleagues may look like:

- telling a colleague you don't want to discuss something personal (e.g. 'I am not comfortable discussing that.')

- not wanting to attend after-work drinks (e.g. 'I would love to come but I have commitments at home tonight.')

- telling a colleague they are getting too close and are in your personal space (e.g. 'Can you please give me a little bit of space?')

- not engaging if a colleague is talking inappropriately about another colleague (e.g. 'I don't feel comfortable engaging in this conversation. Can we talk about something else please?').

If your boundaries are not being respected at work, raise these issues through the appropriate channel. This could be through your direct manager or the human resources department.

WHAT TO DO IF SOMEONE CROSSES YOUR BOUNDARY

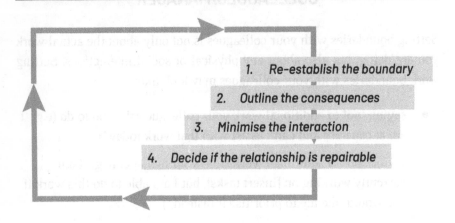

1. Re-establish the boundary
2. Outline the consequences
3. Minimise the interaction
4. Decide if the relationship is repairable

Once you have set boundaries, it can feel incredibly frustrating if they are being consistently ignored and violated. In these situations, it is important to remember that boundaries are made up of standards, actions and outcomes. If the appropriate actions are not being taken to your standard, the outcome is not being met.

1. RE-ESTABLISH THE BOUNDARY

This step is completely optional. You have no obligation to re-establish your boundaries more than once if the person has intentionally ignored your previous discussion and request. If you feel it is suitable for your situation, re-establish your boundary and explain to them again how you feel.

2. OUTLINE THE CONSEQUENCES

When your boundary is crossed, you need to follow this up by outlining a consequence to make it clear that your boundaries are not flexible or up for negotiation. Not doing this will send the message that you will tolerate their actions.

For example:

> *I have already asked you to stop doing that, so please respect my boundary. If you do it again, I am going to leave.*

> *I have already told you that I don't appreciate you talking to me like that. If you continue, I will have to raise this with HR.*

3. MINIMISE THE INTERACTION

There are instances when, despite your best efforts to effectively convey a boundary, the other person is simply not able to respect it. The problem, however, is that you may continue to see this person, either at work, because you are part of the same group of friends or for any other reason. Cutting them off may not be possible. In this scenario, your only option is to minimise your interactions with them as much as you can. Avoid any direct communication with them and keep your distance when physically near each other.

4. DECIDE IF THE RELATIONSHIP IS REPAIRABLE

Minimising interaction may not be the solution to your situation. If someone is repeatedly crossing your boundaries, even after re-establishing them, you will need to decide whether this relationship is repairable. Ask yourself: Is this person making any effort to change their behaviour? Do I feel they truly understand where I am coming from? Do they respect me? Do they want to continue this relationship? Depending on these answers, you may decide the relationship is repairable or you may choose to end the relationship.

HOW TO REACT IF YOU CROSS SOMEONE'S BOUNDARY

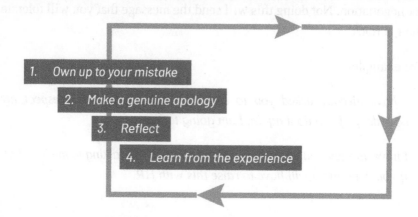

1. Own up to your mistake
2. Make a genuine apology
3. Reflect
4. Learn from the experience

While you may never intend to cross someone else's boundary, it can happen. Now that you understand the importance of boundaries, it is equally important that you respect other people's personal boundaries as well. If you do find yourself accidentally crossing someone's boundary, follow the four steps.

1. OWN UP TO YOUR MISTAKE

First things first: admit fault and acknowledge your mistake. Take all emotion out of it, avoid making excuses and accept responsibility.

2. MAKE A GENUINE APOLOGY

When making an apology, say sorry and acknowledge what happened. Explain to the person how you will move forward to correct this in the future, so it does not happen again.

3. REFLECT

Consider the other person's point of view and think about why the boundary exists. This may give you an appreciation for their position, which may come into your mind next time you are in a similar situation.

4. LEARN FROM THE EXPERIENCE

Think about what you can do differently next time so this doesn't happen again. Run through the scenario in your head again, and decide what you would have said or done differently to avoid crossing this boundary.

SET BOUNDARIES WITH SOCIAL MEDIA

- Unfollow accounts that make you feel bad about yourself

- Post photos that bring you joy, not to seek approval

- Set time limits on scrolling social media apps

- Don't check social media as soon as you wake up

- Mute/block your ex so you don't stalk them

SWS

Many of us spend hours every day on social media — whether that's watching YouTube videos, scrolling through TikTok or gathering inspiration on Pinterest. The endless stream of content sucks you in, and you often lose track of how much time you have spent scrolling. I have a love/hate relationship with social media. On one hand, it's an amazing way to stay connected with friends and family, learn new things and create connections all around the world. But on the other hand, the constant 'highlights reel' content we consume can result in us comparing ourselves to strangers online and feeling self-conscious, unworthy and jealous.

Setting boundaries with your social media usage ensures that you do not let it take over your life or compromise your mental or physical health. Take a step back and assess how you are using your social media accounts and whether it has a positive or negative effect on you. If you find yourself spending hours on Instagram, set a time limit to only check it for 30 minutes a day. If you're always checking in on your ex's profile to see if they've posted something new, block their account for as long as you need to focus on yourself post break-up and heal.

HOW TO HAVE A DIGITAL DETOX

Remove your work emails from your phone

Designate 'device-free' times

Stay off your phone 30 minutes before bed or when you first wake up

Set time limits on your social media usage

Put your phone away when spending time with loved ones

Turn off notifications

Between your phone, smart watch, tablet, computer and TV, it has become almost impossible to not rely on technology to get through our days. In between all of the essential uses, finding time to have a digital detox can give your mind a break from the flashing lights and endless scrolling.

Start slowly by picking one of these tips to implement. Maybe you'll limit yourself to one hour on social media a day or maybe you'll delete the email app off your phone. As you break down your dependence on your digital devices, try and have an entire 'device-free' day on the weekend to clear your mind, be present in the moment and focus on the world around you.

16

Friendships

FRIENDSHIP: GREEN FLAGS VS RED FLAGS

GREEN FLAGS

Always has your back

Great listener and gives the best advice

Genuinely interested in your life

Supports you and helps you grow

Has seen you at your worst and never judges

Asks questions to better understand what you're dealing with

RED FLAGS

Self-centred and creates drama

Constantly puts you down

Never happy for your success

Takes advantage of you

Gossips about you to mutual friends

Projects their insecurities onto you

You may have heard the terms 'red flag' and 'green flag' used to describe both friendships and relationships. But what do these terms actually mean? Like a red traffic light or a red card in a sporting match, a red flag typically signifies a reason to stop. In a relationship context, they serve as a warning sign that it is highly unlikely that you will be able to have a healthy and conflict-free friendship or relationship with this person. Conversely, green flags are the exact opposite and signify reasons to proceed. They are positive traits that indicate that a person can engage in a healthy, mature and supportive friendship or relationship.

The people you choose to surround yourself with play an important role in your success and happiness. Friendships provide the physical, emotional and social support we need as we go through the ups and downs that life throws our way. In the same way that great friends motivate, inspire, support and care for us on our journeys, there are toxic friendships that we may develop that drain our energy and hold us back from achieving our goals.

FRIENDSHIP GREEN FLAGS

ALWAYS HAS YOUR BACK

If you have ever found yourself in a tough life situation, think back to the people who never left your side and were there for you through it all. These friends are loyal and will stand by you when things are not going your way.

GREAT LISTENER AND GIVES THE BEST ADVICE

Sometimes you need to talk about what is on your mind, and a great friend will be there to listen. When it's the right time, they will provide advice and help you see clearly when you are caught up in the emotion of a situation.

GENUINELY INTERESTED IN YOUR LIFE

Your friends should have a genuine interest in your life. They should be clapping for you through life's big moments and providing support through the not-so-great times. They are genuinely curious and want to know what is going on in your life without having to be prompted.

SUPPORTS YOU AND HELPS YOU GROW

A supportive friend appreciates you for who you are and encourages you to pursue your goals. In times when your limiting beliefs are holding you back from making that decision to take that new job opportunity or bounce back after a break-up, a good friend will keep it real and remind you of all your amazing qualities and skills.

HAS SEEN YOU AT YOUR WORST AND NEVER JUDGES

A best friend can see you at your absolute lowest point and will never judge you. No matter what, they stick by you even if they do not agree with your decision or your values may not align. With that being said, a true friend needs to be honest and fair. Their honesty comes from a place of support and wanting what's best for you and your wellbeing. They aren't afraid to give you painful truths if it is for your greater good. Be wary of friends who claim to be honest but do not have your best intentions at heart. These people are not your real friends and their comments come from a place of jealousy and resentment.

ASKS QUESTIONS TO BETTER UNDERSTAND
WHAT YOU'RE DEALING WITH

Whenever you are going through a challenging time or facing a tough decision, a good friend will ask questions to better understand what you are dealing with so they can support you and provide appropriate assistance. They will not dismiss you by making comments such as: 'You'll be fine', 'You're over-reacting' or 'Stop making a big deal out of it. It's nothing'. Instead, they will provide you with a safe space to share your thoughts and feelings.

FRIENDSHIP RED FLAGS

SELF-CENTRED AND CREATES DRAMA

A big red flag is when a person expects all conversations to be about them. Their problems are always more important than yours, and they rarely (or never) ask about what you are going through. When you do bring something up, their typical response is: 'That's not as bad as what happened to me'. They constantly create drama and every week there is a new argument, dilemma or issue with someone in their life.

CONSTANTLY PUTS YOU DOWN

If a person belittles you, makes you feel insignificant and criticises everything you do or say, they are not your friend. Whether the person is doing it intentionally or not, being constantly put down diminishes your confidence and self-worth.

NEVER HAPPY FOR YOUR SUCCESS

A supportive friend will always celebrate your achievements and cheer you on every step of the way. If you achieve a huge milestone and notice some of your friends stay silent, it may be a sign that they are jealous as they now see you as a threat or competition that they must outdo.

TAKES ADVANTAGE OF YOU

Friendship is a two-way street. It is a red flag when someone always asks you for help or a favour, but never reciprocates when you need something. While you can't expect your friends to always drop everything when you need them, if you are providing more to the friendship than you are receiving for a prolonged period of time, you may be getting taken advantage of.

GOSSIPS ABOUT YOU TO MUTUAL FRIENDS

Another red flag when it comes to friendships are people who constantly talk poorly or spread gossip about others, including their so-called 'friends'. They are quick to judge others behind their back, but will show a different face in person. If this person always gossips about others, it's a safe assumption they're gossiping about you to others.

PROJECTS THEIR INSECURITIES ONTO YOU

Reminiscing and laughing about old embarrassing stories with your friends is an enjoyable part of any catch-up. It crosses the line when someone always brings up the same story about something that they know you are insecure about. This turns good-natured banter between friends into demeaning and negging insults. Often this is a reflection of their own insecurities that they are projecting onto you.

HOW TO STRENGTHEN YOUR FRIENDSHIPS

Share a meme/photo/ memory that made you think of them

Try new experiences together

Learn your friendship love languages

Don't be afraid to be vulnerable

Check in with them regularly

Show interest in their work, hobbies and goals

Remind them how much they mean to you

Friends have a significant impact on our lives and overall happiness. They help you celebrate the good times and are there by your side to support you through the bad times. They make you feel like you belong and boost your self-confidence. They keep you accountable and encourage you to pursue your goals.

As we get older and are faced with many competing priorities, such as work and children, our friendships can take a back seat. Finding a true friend is rare, and it is important to invest time and effort to strengthen, develop and maintain the friendship. Focus on quality over quantity and follow these tips to nurture the friendships that mean the most to you.

CONSISTENCY

Consistency is one of the most important elements in maintaining and strengthening any friendship. There are several ways to maintain communication and contact with a friend: phone calls, texts, emails, in-person catch-ups or tagging each other in content online. No matter your preferred communication style, what is important is that you do so regularly. Checking in regularly with a friend gives you the chance to reconnect and provide support to one another. It can be as simple as sending a quick text saying:

How was your day?

I saw this and thought of you straight away! How have you been?

Is there anything I can do to help you?

Remember when (share a memory/photo)

Checking in regularly with a friend gives you the chance to reconnect and provide support to one another.

VULNERABILITY

The ability to be vulnerable and honest with a friend builds trust and allows both parties to connect on a deeper level. This does not necessarily mean telling someone your deepest secrets, but being able to express how you are feeling and what you are going through in a safe environment.

POSITIVITY

Friendships are built on positive experiences and supporting each other through difficult times. To maintain a strong friendship, avoid letting negativity, judgement or comparisons enter into your dialogue. Compliment your friends, tell them what an amazing job they are doing and reaffirm that you are there for them if they need any support.

Strengthening a friendship often begins with getting to know more about them. Asking questions about their interests, hobbies, family or job will give them the opportunity to open up and connect with you on a deeper level. Take an interest in their life and show up for them wherever possible. If they have a big event on for work or they mentioned something they were excited about, make a note to check in and see how it went.

MEANINGFUL COMPLIMENTS TO GIVE TO SOMEONE

'You look so happy.'

'You always put me in a better mood.'

'You have the best energy.'

'I'm so lucky to have met you.'

'You are so fun to be around.'

'I wish there were more people like you.'

'You are a great listener.'

'You inspire me.'

A compliment has the power to change somebody's day and inspire a positive change in their life. It is no surprise that we still remember random compliments or kind words that we received days, weeks or even years ago. Compliments boost our self-esteem and ignite positive self-talk in our minds. When someone compliments you on something you typically don't feel confident in, your mind starts to question the validity and truth behind your self-doubt. Receiving praise from an external party can help you believe in the unique talents and strengths you have.

Compliments go beyond the workplace or our physical appearance. There are a variety of meaningful compliments that you can give to someone about their personality, energy and how they make you feel. After reading this page, call, text or email a friend, loved one or colleague and give them a compliment. I promise you, it will bring the biggest smile to their face.

17

Relationships

RELATIONSHIP: GREEN FLAGS VS RED FLAGS

GREEN FLAGS

Willing to make compromises

Clear communication

Makes you a priority in their life

Supports you and helps you grow

Trust, honesty and loyalty

You respect each other's boundaries

RED FLAGS

Emotionally unavailable

Attacks and lies to you

Doesn't respect you or listen to your feelings

Takes no responsibility for their own behaviour

Never there for you when you need them

Acts like the only person who matters

A relationship red flag is a warning sign that indicates you will unlikely be able to have a healthy and conflict-free relationship with this person. A relationship green flag, on the other hand, is a positive trait that indicates that a person can engage in a healthy, mature and supportive relationship. It is often easy to be swept off our feet in the early stages of dating, which can lead us to ignore red flags and inappropriate behaviours. Being conscious of common relationship red flags will allow you to identify them more easily and know the minimum standards and values a potential partner must meet.

RELATIONSHIP GREEN FLAGS

WILLING TO MAKE COMPROMISES

A healthy relationship involves making compromises. It means coming together with your partner to reach a place of understanding on important topics, such as where you live, how you will spend your time or money, how you allocate household chores or how you raise your children. It's about finding a healthy balance where both you and your partner feel heard and can come to an effective solution. Having a partner who is willing to compromise fosters trust and deepens your connection.

CLEAR COMMUNICATION

A healthy relationship relies on clear communication. Effective communication involves both listening and speaking to communicate your needs, opinions, feelings and thoughts. This could be simple things, like sharing how your day was or making plans for the weekend, or more serious issues, like discussing something they did or said that upset you. Having open lines of communication means you won't have to guess what your partner is thinking and can tackle minor issues before they escalate into something bigger.

MAKES YOU A PRIORITY IN THEIR LIFE

Another green flag when entering a relationship is when your partner makes you a priority in their life. This does not mean spending every waking minute together. It simply means that they make an effort to have quality time together and make you feel heard, wanted and desired. There are many different ways that your partner can show they are prioritising you. This may be by having a set date night every week that you never miss, always watching the latest episode of your favourite show together or putting your phones away during dinner to give each other your full attention. Whatever it may be, feeling like you are an important part of your partner's life is a positive sign.

SUPPORTS YOU AND HELPS YOU GROW

Your partner should be your biggest fan (besides yourself, of course). Their positive support will give you the confidence you need to get through the bad days and appreciate the good days. Your partner will push you to stay committed to your personal growth and keep you accountable as you work towards your goals.

People in healthy relationships have both shared dreams and individual dreams of their own. A lot of people get scared that they will have to push their dreams to the side when entering into a new relationship, but this is not the case at all. They should be cheering you on to go for your individual goals, and you should be supporting them in achieving theirs. Regularly discussing your goals and how you can achieve them helps you feel more connected as a couple.

TRUST, HONESTY AND LOYALTY

Building trust and loyalty is the foundation of all relationships. It allows a relationship to develop and grow with a mutual commitment to each other. You should never need to deceive, hide the truth or misdirect your partner. A transparent and honest relationship means the truth is always spoken. Maintaining a healthy relationship requires you both to remain honest in both your actions, as well as your thoughts and feelings.

YOU RESPECT EACH OTHER'S BOUNDARIES

As we discussed in chapter 15, boundaries are an essential part of any healthy relationship. Setting clear boundaries creates guidelines for your partner for how you would like to be treated and the standards of behaviour that you will accept.

It is a green flag if your partner respects your boundaries without questioning them or pushing back on them. Similarly, you should also respect their boundaries. Doing so builds greater trust and safety between you both.

RELATIONSHIP RED FLAGS

EMOTIONALLY UNAVAILABLE

Your partner should be open and honest about their emotions, expressing how they feel about themselves and your relationship. A relationship becomes stronger if there is a deeper connection through open dialogue about each other's emotions. You are unable to understand the needs of your partner without this expression. If your partner is unable to open themselves up emotionally to you, you will not be able to build the foundations of a healthy relationship.

ATTACKS AND LIES TO YOU

Dishonesty and unreasonable conflict in a relationship are unhealthy traits that develop into serious relationship deal-breakers. Continuous lying, whether big or small, removes any possibility that a trusting and honest relationship can be built. This includes your partner keeping secrets about themselves or being vague about important information that impacts your relationship. Further, steer clear of people who resort to passive-aggressive and blaming behaviour whenever a difficult situation or conflict arises. If your choices and actions are met with constant attacking criticism, you will be left to feel inadequate and unworthy.

DOESN'T RESPECT YOU OR LISTEN TO YOUR FEELINGS

Mutual respect and understanding for each other are some of the most fundamental components of a relationship. Reflect on your relationship and ask yourself the following questions: Are you consulted before a big decision is made? Do you get put down and embarrassed in social settings? Are the things you explain are important to you diminished and avoided? If you answered 'yes' to any of the above, it may be time to reconsider your relationship. Someone who dismisses your emotions, belittles you or makes you feel insignificant is not a person you want to be with.

TAKES NO RESPONSIBILITY FOR THEIR OWN BEHAVIOUR

Generally, when you do or say something that upsets your partner, the correct process is to admit fault, apologise and work on changing your behaviour so it does not happen again. However, this is not the case if you are dating someone who is unable to take responsibility for their behaviour. When you question their actions, they either lie about it, deny any wrongdoing or gaslight you. People like this lack the emotional maturity to be in a relationship, and you will struggle to resolve conflicts that inevitably arise. You cannot change a person or force them to hold themselves accountable.

NEVER THERE FOR YOU WHEN YOU NEED THEM

You should always be able to depend on and count on your partner. They are the person you should be able to turn to in a moment of crisis to provide comfort, safety and support. A supportive partner will do everything they can to be there both physically and emotionally through important events in your life. They do not ignore you, dismiss you or take a step back when you need them the most.

ACTS LIKE THE ONLY PERSON WHO MATTERS

You can never be in a relationship with someone who is selfish and only cares about themselves. All conversations centre around them, all decisions are made by them, and your input or opinion is never considered or given any regard. This self-centredness dismisses your feelings and chips away at your self-worth, making you feel isolated and ignored in the relationship. There is no reciprocation of the physical and emotional effort that you put into the relationship to meet their needs.

LOVE SOUNDS LIKE...

'I am so proud of you.'

'How can I help you?'

'You are perfect exactly how you are.'

'You mean the world to me.'

'I believe in you.'

'Let's work through this together.'

'Drive safely.'

'I was wrong.'

'I didn't know you felt that way. I'm sorry.'

'How was your day?'

'I respect your boundaries.'

'I am always here for you.'

'I'll take care of this.'

'You are amazing.'

There are many different ways to express your care and love for a person, in addition to 'I love you'. This could involve:

- asking them about their day
- showing genuine interest in them
- listening to their problems and offering advice
- admitting when you are at fault
- not being afraid to apologise
- providing encouragement and words of support
- making sure they feel safe and heard
- reassuring them that you are on the same team.

Every relationship is unique, and love can look and sound very different to different people. However, what is consistent across all loving relationships is that they are rooted in kindness, commitment, support, safety, reassurance, understanding and comfort.

HOW TO SHOW LOVE TO YOUR PARTNER

Compliment or encourage them

Tell them why you love them

Send an unexpected loving text/note

Make them breakfast/dinner

Help with any chores or errands

Hugs, kisses and cuddling

Offer a massage

Put your phone away and give your full attention

Go for a walk

Plan date nights

Listen

Fresh flowers

Small surprise gifts

Make birthdays/anniversaries special

Expressing love to and receiving love from your partner is an essential component to maintaining a strong, long-lasting relationship. What is difficult, however, is learning how to express your love in a way that your partner appreciates. Everyone has their own preferences when it comes to receiving affection. For some, they may like to receive unexpected loving texts or a heartfelt card with words of encouragement and support. For others, planning a special date night where you both put your phones away and give each other your full attention is the way they feel most connected.

If you are not sure how your partner prefers to receive love and affection, ask them and have a conversation about it. You may be surprised at the simple things that they appreciate you doing. Start picking up cues along the way as well. If your partner is feeling down and you ask how you can help, listen carefully to their response. If they want to curl up in bed together watching a movie or to go out for a morning walk, you can start to understand the different types of affection they most enjoy. No matter what, all types of expression of love have one thing in common: they intend to make the other person feel valued and appreciated.

QUESTIONS TO DEEPEN YOUR CONNECTION WITH YOUR PARTNER

- If you could write a note to your younger self, what would you say in only three words?

- When is the last time you cried?

- Do you believe everything happens for a reason, or do we just find reasons after things happen?

- What should a healthy relationship provide for the people in it?

- Which is truer: that social media makes us closer together or that it makes us feel more alone?

- In your life, what has been the biggest blessing in disguise?

- What would you do with your life if you were suddenly given a billion dollars?

- Do you usually follow your head or your heart when making decisions?

- Is there anything you consider absolutely unforgivable?

- If you could pick one year of your life to do over, which would it be and why?

HEALTHY RELATIONSHIP TECHNIQUES

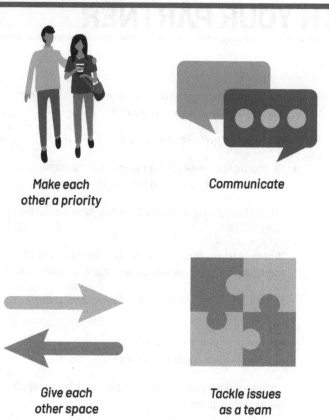

Make each
other a priority

Communicate

Give each
other space

Tackle issues
as a team

No relationship is ever sunshine and rainbows 100 per cent of the time. Even the 'perfect' couples you see online have problems and issues. Conflict, disagreements, rough patches and slumps are all completely normal parts of a relationship. There's a reason why the term 'honeymoon period' exists. When we first start dating someone new, everything seems carefree, easy and happy. But as the newness of the relationship wears off, and you are faced with the emotions and stresses of everyday life, things may start to change. You start discovering their deeper personality traits or habits. Their little quirks that you initially found cute may start to annoy you. This is not a reason to panic, and it's a natural stage of any relationship as you become more comfortable with each other and more intertwined. What's important is that you engage in healthy relationship techniques to stay connected and strong no matter what comes your way. Remember: you are not only a couple, but also a team.

MAKE EACH OTHER A PRIORITY

One of the best ways to maintain a strong relationship is to always make each other your top priority. Remind your partner frequently what you love about them and how much they mean to you. Keep flirting like you just met and be spontaneous whenever possible. It can be easy to get stuck in a routine after you have been together for a while, but keep things fresh by planning fun date nights and surprising each other. Bring home their favourite dessert, book tickets to a movie they've been dying to see or write them a surprise note.

COMMUNICATE

Communication is essential to stay connected in your relationship. Talk regularly and honestly about everything, such as how your day was, what you dreamed about, your random thoughts, plans you have for the weekend or a video that made you laugh. Keep them up to date about what is happening at your workplaces and show interest in what they are working on.

If your partner has had a bad day, a simple question that works wonders is: 'Do you want to vent or do you want advice?' This gives them the opportunity to communicate the best way for you to support them in that moment. On a similar note, if your partner has done something that has upset you or is bothering you, don't go silent or start being passive-aggressive. Bring up the issue openly and talk through it together.

GIVE EACH OTHER SPACE

Everyone needs alone time, and you do not need to be with your partner every spare minute of your day. Spending time apart to re-energise and relax is not a bad thing. Similarly, encourage your partner to maintain their hobbies and regularly see and hang out with their friends. Not only will this ensure that you maintain a sense of independence within your relationship, but it will also give you time to miss them and have more things to talk about when you are together.

TACKLE ISSUES AS A TEAM

Whenever you face a problem with your partner or within your relationship, remember this: It is never you vs your partner. It is always you and your partner vs the problem. Keep any problems you have between the two of you. Avoid gossiping about your partner, ranting to or getting any friends or family involved unless absolutely necessary. This can make the situation more complicated and takes the focus outside of the two people in the relationship working through the issue together.

HOW TO APOLOGISE

1	Take responsibility	'I did x.'
2	Admit fault	'I'm sorry, I was wrong.'
3	Name the impact	'I hurt you.'
4	Do not use the word 'if'	'I'm sorry if I hurt you.'
5	Don't shift the blame/defend	'But you did y.'
6	Don't use the passive voice	'Sorry if you were offended.'
7	Make amends	'In future, I will ...'

Learning how to give a proper apology is one of the most under-rated skills in life. We all make mistakes. What is key is understanding how to take ownership of your mistake, learn from it and use the experience as a way to grow closer with your partner, friend, colleague or loved one. A genuine apology also communicates to the other person that you are mature enough to manage conflict in a healthy way and do not want the situation to occur again in the future.

A genuine apology always starts with taking responsibility for your actions (or inaction). This means openly acknowledging your mistake that hurt the other person. Do not try to shift the blame or defend your actions. Admit fault and express your regret about the situation. The other person should know that you feel remorseful for hurting them and that you wish it didn't happen. Never imply that it is not your fault by using words like 'if' or passive voice in your apology. Finish off by clarifying the actions you will take to move forward and ensure that the same thing does not occur again. This shows that you have learned from the experience and will, hopefully, be able to regain their trust.

WHAT TO SAY WHEN SOMEONE IS UPSET

'What is the best way I can support you right now?'

'We don't have to talk about it right now. Let's do x instead.'

'If you are comfortable, tell me what happened. How did that make you feel?'

'I'm always here to listen if you want to talk.'

When we see someone who is upset, our instinct is to console them. However, we are often unsure of the best way to do this, and don't want to run the risk of saying or doing the wrong thing and making them more upset. The best way to react will depend on the specific situation and the reasons why the person is upset in the first place.

Sometimes less is more in these situations. Before any words are spoken, sitting down next to them and, if appropriate and accepted, wrapping your arm around them might be the thing that they need in that moment. Express that you are there to support them and listen to them if they want to talk about the situation. Offer advice if they want to receive it. Sometimes they just want someone to listen to them, and at other times, they want help to solve or move forward with the situation. In other circumstances, the best way to support someone is by helping them take their mind off the situation. This could be talking about their favourite hobby or going out for a walk to your favourite coffee shop.

If you're not sure of the best way to support your loved one, ask them. If they say they want some space, respect their wishes and be there for them when they need you. Everyone processes their emotions differently, and the best thing you can do as a friend is offer support, love and kindness.

OVERCOMING A BREAK-UP

Cut off contact

Re-establish your priorities

Make a list

Get social

Focus on healing

Break-ups suck. No matter if you were the initiator, caught off guard or if it was mutual, heartbreak is one of the worst pains and feelings you can experience. Even if you have gone through a break-up before, it never gets any easier, and we all process and heal from it differently. Nonetheless, there are a few processes to work through to try and overcome the break-up effectively.

CUT OFF CONTACT

Break-up rule number one: cut off all contact. Even if you had the most amicable break-up, taking this person out of your life (even if this is only for a set period of time) will give you the space to move on and focus on the next chapter of your life.

I get it, it's hard. It could be a random Tuesday night, which was your night to make tacos together, and you suddenly feel the urge to text them and check in. Or you're out with your friends and you keep stalking their Instagram story to see what they're up to. But every time you send them a text, call them, stalk them online or see them in person, you delay your healing.

There is absolutely no benefit to staying up to date with their life through social media or by catching up for coffee to see how they have been. Mute, block, delete or avoid your ex for as long as you need to heal. You don't need to apologise to them or give any explanations. Keeping in touch, either in person, digitally or socially, makes it difficult for your mind to let them go. You will continue to feel attached to your ex and dwell on what could have been.

MAKE A LIST

After a break-up, we have a tendency to shine a light on all the good memories, times and moments shared with our ex, while glossing over all of the issues and problems that existed in the relationship. Grab two sheets of paper. On one sheet of paper, make a list of all the things that did work in your relationship. On the other sheet of paper, make a list of all the things that didn't work. Be brutally honest with yourself. Write down specific memories and moments where you were upset, argued, felt betrayed or didn't feel safe and loved. Write down the character traits you didn't like or values they held that you disagree with.

Compare the lists. Look at the 'what didn't work' list every day as you venture through your healing process. Does the list make you realise that they were nowhere near perfect? That you didn't like a lot of the things they did or said? Did you love them just enough to overlook these things and accept them? Conversely, hide the 'what worked' list. One day, when you're ready, this will be your list for your next relationship. It'll remind you of the values you want to bring along to make sure that you are taking care of your needs when you enter into a new romance.

FOCUS ON HEALING

Healing a break-up takes time and it is not a linear process. Some days will be bad, and you'll struggle getting out of bed or miss them so much that your heart physically aches. Other days will be better, and you'll start to feel stronger and ready to move forward with your life.

Your self-esteem may be quite low post-break-up, especially if your partner initiated the break-up. You may be questioning what went wrong, what is wrong with you and whether you will ever find love again. Practising positive affirmations is a helpful tool to overcome any negative self-talk. Repeating phrases such as 'This break-up was not my fault', 'I am worthy of love' and 'I will grow and learn from this experience' helps your subconscious mind adopt healthy thought patterns and starts the process of healing.

Take the time to forgive yourself for any mistakes you may have made, for giving away your power, for past behaviours or actions, for the guilt that you may feel or simply for the difficult time you had to go through. This is not about letting your ex off the hook for anything they did; it's about your own internal forgiveness and emotional freedom. Forgiving yourself is a powerful tool to expel any self-rejection and replace it with self-acceptance and self-love. It is only when you release these tensions that you can move on.

RE-ESTABLISH YOUR PRIORITIES

Rightly or wrongly, your relationship may have caused you to place a hold on some of your priorities. Take this opportunity to re-establish these priorities. This may be your love for the arts, applying for that new role at work or focusing on your self-care routine. Make a list of the top priorities you now have coming out of this relationship and how you plan to address each one. Set boundaries with yourself and the people around you to ensure you protect your peace and focus solely on the priorities you have set out.

GET SOCIAL

It can be tempting to not leave the house post-break-up and stay rugged-up on the couch eating ice cream and watching sad movies. While this is a key step in your healing process, there comes a time where you need to leave the house and bring some fun back into your life. Getting social post-break-up is a great way to rebuild your confidence and self-esteem. Say yes to spontaneous activities with friends, meeting new people and trying new things.

BREAK-UP REMINDERS

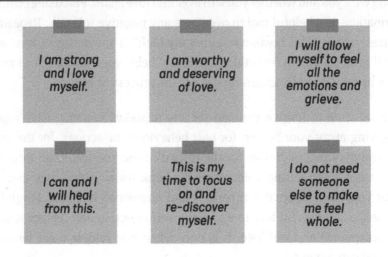

I am strong and I love myself.

I am worthy and deserving of love.

I will allow myself to feel all the emotions and grieve.

I can and I will heal from this.

This is my time to focus on and re-discover myself.

I do not need someone else to make me feel whole.

As they say, time heals everything. Unfortunately, there is no crystal ball or methodical rule that will tell you how much time you need to heal from your break-up, but one thing that is for certain is that it will be an incredible period of self-discovery, reflection and personal growth.

As you work through your healing process, come back to this page as often as you need. Say these reminders out loud. Write them down on a post-it note and stick it to your computer. Repeat the affirmations on your good days and even more on the days where you think you'll never feel better. While it may feel like you'll never get through this, I promise you that you will.

HOW TO BE HAPPY BEING SINGLE

- Release any pressures
- Focus on yourself
- Strengthen your non-romantic relationships

Being single gets a bad rap. In movies, single characters are often depicted as being sad and lonely, longing for a partner to sweep them off their feet into a better, happier life. But it doesn't have to be that way. We should reframe being single as one of the most empowering times in our lives: a time where you can be selfish, prioritise your own needs and choose how you spend your time and who you spend that time with.

RELEASE ANY PRESSURES

Being single or in a relationship does not define your value as a person. Society pushes the idea that being in a relationship is an essential part of living a happy life. But you are not less worthy simply because you are not in a relationship. Do not allow internal or external pressures to find a partner or get married or have kids convince you otherwise.

Even worse, don't allow these pressures to push you into a mediocre relationship that you don't want to be in. Never rush into a relationship, and do not settle simply because you feel lonely or guilty that you are single. Relationships take a lot of your time and energy, so you need to make sure you are investing in the right one. On top of that, settling for just any relationship can lead to accepting toxic behaviours and ignoring red flags.

What's most important is that you are truly happy within yourself and living your life in accordance with your goals and values. If a partner comes along and can add to your life, that's amazing. But if they don't, that's also okay, because you know that you have everything within yourself to succeed, flourish and live a fulfilled life.

FOCUS ON YOURSELF

Being single gives you the opportunity to truly invest in yourself. Embrace the fact that you are able to live your life on your own accord. Be selfish with your time and focus on whatever will bring you happiness. Take time to learn more about yourself. What do you enjoy doing? Why do you enjoy doing it? Define your goals and priorities, and think about how you can spend more time pursuing these. This can be anything from taking on a new career direction or simply being more spontaneous and saying 'yes' to new things and opportunities.

STRENGTHEN YOUR NON-ROMANTIC RELATIONSHIPS

A relationship involves a big commitment of time, effort and emotional energy. Redirect the time and energy that you would put into a relationship towards strengthening your friendships and other non-romantic relationships instead. Make a conscious effort to check in with them regularly, organise catch-ups, have a laugh and some fun, provide support and ask for help when needed. Cultivating strong friendships and non-romantic relationships boosts your self-confidence, happiness and fulfillment in life.

FIRST DATE CONVERSATION STARTERS

QUESTION	WHY
What does your typical day look like?	You will gain an understanding of their habits, routines, priorities, what they do for work and how they spend their free time after work and on weekends.
Where did you grow up (and what was it like there)?	You will gain insight into their upbringing and can bond over any similarities or learn more about any differences.
What is something you're trying to learn?	You will learn more about their hobbies and understand their pursuit for growth and personal development.
What is your dream job?	You will learn about their aspirations and values.
If you could travel anywhere right now, where would you go?	You will learn more about their interests, ideal types of holidays and you can share travel stories.
What's on your bucket list?	This is a fun question to discover their interests and passions.

There are very few things more nerve-wracking than a first date. Questioning what to wear, where to go and hoping that there are no awkward silences or pauses in conversation. You may have spoken in the lead-up before the date or you may barely know each other. A first date is meant to be a fun way to get to know someone new and see if you are compatible. The best way to do this is by asking open-ended questions that will ignite deeper conversation. Next time you go on a first date (or second or third or...), try out these questions. You'll gain a deeper understanding of the other person, their values, their goals and their aspirations.

FINAL THOUGHTS

If you have reached this page, congratulations! We covered a lot of ground in this book, and I hope you have been able to implement some of the tips in your own life.

As I said at the very start, don't let this book collect dust on your bookshelf. Come back to it as often as you need. Use it as your handbook as you navigate adult life.

I want to leave you with one final reminder.

You are capable of so much more than you think.

Ignore that voice inside your head that convinces you that you're not.

Let go of the limiting beliefs that hold you back.

Ignore the negative opinions of others who try to make you feel small.

Stop doubting yourself.

You are strong, smart and brave, and will overcome any challenge that comes your way.

Take charge.

Take control.

Your dream life is waiting for you.

Your no. 1 fan,

Téa